Zero tolerance policing

Maurice Punch

First published in Great Britain in 2007 by The Policy Press

The Policy Press
University of Bristol
Fourth Floor, Beacon House
Queen's Road
Bristol BS8 1QU
UK

Tel no +44 (0)117 331 4054
Fax no +44 (0)117 331 4093
E-mail tpp-info@bristol.ac.uk
www.policypress.org.uk

ISBN 978 1 84742 055 8

British Library Cataloguing in Publication Data
A catalogue record for this report is available from the British Library.

Library of Congress Cataloging-in-Publication Data
A catalog record for this report has been requested.

Cover image courtesy of iStockphoto®
Cover design by Qube Design Associates, Bristol
Printed in Great Britain by Latimer Trend, Plymouth

To the memory of Colin Cramphorn and Tom Williamson

Contents

Preface

From the mid-1970s onwards, I became acquainted with the criminal justice world in the Netherlands through research, teaching and conferences. I conducted research in Amsterdam in the period 1974-80 (Punch, 1979a, 1985), taught Dutch police officers until the mid-1980s and later became involved in projects with the police in Utrecht and Amsterdam. In 1995 I helped to write *Toekomst Gezocht* for the Dutch Police Foundation for Society and Safety (SMVP, 1995) which was published in translation as *Searching for a Future* (Punch et al, 1998); the Dutch Police had just been through a major reorganisation, there was something of a loss of direction and this work presented a perspective for policing in the future. More recently, I have concentrated on developments in policing in the UK and the US. Two years ago, I received an assignment from the Police Research Programme (Programma Politie en Wetenschap, which is funded by the Dutch Ministry of the Interior in The Hague) on the 'transfer' of zero tolerance policing from abroad. This volume is based on the Dutch report for that project, Punch (2006a) *Van 'Alles Mag' Naar 'Zero Tolerance': Policy Transfer en de Nederlandse Politie* (Apeldoorn: Programma Politie en Wetenschap/Police Research Programme), and quotations are from the unpublished English version, Punch (2006b) entitled From 'Anything Goes' to 'Zero Tolerance': Policy Transfer and the Dutch Police. The director of the programme has kindly allowed me to incorporate parts of that English text into this work. The full English report is available from me (punch@xs4all.nl), and the Dutch version from www.politieenwetenschap.nl.

Acknowledgements

I am most grateful to a number of Dutch police chiefs, politicians and academics whom I was able to interview for the research. Furthermore, I greatly appreciate the valuable comments on drafts of my original report from Frits Vlek, Kees van der Vijver, René van Swaaningen, Bob Hoogenboom, Geert de Vries and Alexis Aronowitz (in the Netherlands); Tim Newburn, David Downes, Ben Bowling, Robert Reiner, Mercedes Hinton, Tank Waddington, Stan Gilmour and Paul Rock (in Britain); and Peter Manning and Peter Moskos (in the US). I have been fortunate in the quality, and mildness, of my commentators, some of whom (for example, Barry Loveday) also provided me with copies of their published or unpublished work in this area. I am also indebted to Mike Hough for critically reading this work with a view to publication.

Finally, I was greatly helped with my thoughts on policing in general and zero tolerance in particular by a number of 'reflective practitioners', including Geoffrey Markham (former Assistant Chief Constable, Essex Police), and Colin Cramphorn and Tom Williamson, who have both sadly passed away. All three held strong but considered views on policing and were sceptical of the zero tolerance approach, feeling that it leaned towards repression.

Colin Cramphorn, former Chief Constable of West Yorkshire Police, was a dynamic and perceptive police leader who was widely liked and respected within the service and outside it. The London bombers of 2005 came from his 'patch' and, although he was ill, he worked tirelessly with his officers to keep the peace in the aftermath of the bombings. In relation to 'policy transfer' he felt that going over to America to look at policing developments there was fairly pointless and preferred an exchange relationship with a European Police Force (Utrecht in the Netherlands).

Tom Williamson, former Deputy Chief Constable of Nottinghamshire, became an energetic and productive academic at Portsmouth University following retirement from the police. He was a thoughtful and supportive colleague, had wide interests, was working on several books and was planning a study of the transformation of policing in the UK with me when he became seriously ill. Both were men of principle and they will be sorely missed. I dedicate this book to their memory.

Amstelveen, July 2007

Notes on the author

Maurice Punch has worked at universities in the UK, US and the Netherlands, where he has lived since 1975. He has researched corporate crime, and corruption and reform of the police. He has written on police corruption scandals in several countries, *Conduct Unbecoming* (1985): other published work includes articles in English, Dutch, French and American journals and several books, including *Dirty Business: Exploring Corporate Misconduct* (Sage Publications, 1996). His latest book, with Jim Gobert (University of Essex), is *Rethinking Corporate Crime* (Cambridge University Press, 2003). In 1994, after 18 years in Dutch universities, he became an independent researcher and consultant. Since then, he has continued to research policing and the devious and criminal side of business, to teach senior police officers and to contribute to university programmes for managers and to in-house seminars for executives. He has taken part in numerous conferences, including those for the Council of Europe, the United Nations and the National Institute of Justice. In 1999, he became Visiting Professor at the Mannheim Centre for Criminology, London School of Economics and Political Science where he teaches in graduate courses on policing and corporate crime. He also contributes regularly to the Masters in Criminology programme at King's College London.

Summary

In this examination of British and Dutch interest in American-style zero tolerance policing, I place this policy transfer in relation to influential developments in policing and criminal justice in the wider, even global, environment. Police forces everywhere are under constant pressure to change and have become increasingly internationally oriented; looking at police appraisal of zero tolerance in two societies can inform us of shifting paradigms in policing, policy formulation and implementation in practice. To a large degree, police in both Britain and the Netherlands had traditionally adopted a 'service and consent' model of policing that was particularly strong in the Netherlands. When New York became associated with a new and tougher approach to law enforcement, dubbed 'zero tolerance', it attracted a great deal of attention from abroad, particularly as zero tolerance was held to have led to a substantial reduction in crime. The considerable political and media attention fostered by this can be seen as a periodic return to emphasising the 'crime control' paradigm.

The policing innovations in the US, especially the New York model, also interested large numbers of visitors from abroad, including senior British and Dutch police officers. In both Britain and the Netherlands, however, there was considerable ambivalence, scepticism and even hostility among practitioners to implementing zero tolerance. To understand what was subsequently implemented in these two countries, I have had to unravel the diffuse label zero tolerance and divide it into several components. Some elements – such as techniques associated with information-led policing ('Compstat'), the emphasis on 'fixing broken windows' (solving community problems to reverse decline) and a more assertive and directed police presence on the streets – were adopted. As in much policy transfer, the practitioners, in a pragmatic and even opportunistic manner, filtered out the innovations that could realistically be implemented while endeavouring to fit them into existing values and practices. But in both societies, there was little enthusiasm for the underlying 'tough on crime' mantra. The policing elites in both countries were under pressure to shift to a crime control model, but this no longer fitted with the more balanced, consultative and rights-based approach that had been adopted in recent years.

In retrospect, then, there was no 'Americanisation' of British or Dutch policing: zero tolerance was more of a rhetorical device, driven by politics and the media, than a major policy shift. It was an attractive catch phrase, conveying simplicity and determination, but it was essentially a crude restatement of a traditional crime control model that fitted into a wider shift towards punitiveness in criminal justice in the US. It may well have acted as a catalyst for a more assertive style of policing geared to the swift use of intelligence and a more visible police presence on the streets. But, in essence, while the two examples presented here might be seen as 'failed transfer', they can also be viewed as revealing the resilience of the 'service and consent' paradigm in British and Dutch policing.

Introduction

'God knows, when I came in, an outsider, there were some resistant lieutenants at first. They'd say "What makes you think this shit will work here? What do you know about New Orleans? What the hell do you Yankees think you can tell us?"' (Jack Maple, former New York police officer turned consultant, cited in Remnick, 1997, p 102)

The police organisation has been subject to constant pressure to change during the past two decades. In the UK this has come from successive governments determined to reform the police into an effective and efficient public service. The model to be followed in this reforming campaign was that of management practice in business corporations. And, fed by political interests and intense media attention, a focal element in this near frenetic thrust has been crime reduction. In effect, there has been a 'maelstrom of reform', unrelenting pressure, a battery of shifting demands, constant reorganisations, management training with fresh skills and a new conceptual vocabulary, and the political promise of yet more change to come. Some proposals speak of centralisation, regionalisation, amalgamations, lateral entry and increasing workplace diversity. Ian Blair, then Deputy Commissioner of the Metropolitan Police (or 'Met'), left people in no doubt that the British police service was 'reinventing' itself and that its leaders were up and ready for radical change:

'The police service is sometimes caricatured as the most resistant to change of all public services.... But resistance to change just isn't true. At least, it isn't true of chiefs ... the leaders of the service want a different service from the existing one, are not being pushed towards reform but are leading the way ... the police service is up for reform.' (Blair, 2003)

The landscape of policing in the UK (with some variations in England and Wales, Scotland and Northern Ireland) and elsewhere is, then, being realigned and there is an emphasis on constant innovation, new policy initiatives and fresh concepts. One of these was, and is, 'zero tolerance'. Here I shall examine this notion, which promised a new style of policing, and how it attracted a great deal of attention. In particular, I trace the New York model's crossing of the Atlantic and its 'transfer' to the UK and the Netherlands. But, in order to sketch the context for change in which policing and criminal justice is operating, I outline a set of complex and interwoven factors that have affected policies and practice in the past few decades.

These developments can be divided into 12 key areas (see Morgan and Newburn, 1997; Reiner, 1997, 2000; Newburn, 2003, 2005), as follows.

Neoliberalism President Reagan in the US and Prime Minister Thatcher in the UK espoused so-called 'neoliberal' political and monetarist economic policies that argued for the primacy of markets within the capitalist system, cuts in public spending and welfare systems, and a tougher approach to crime.

Punitiveness The ideology, rhetoric and practice in the US fostered 'punitiveness' in criminal justice with tougher sentencing, 'three strikes and you're out', harsher penal regimes (with 'boot camps' and 'chain gangs') and a more frequent implementation of capital punishment (Tonry, 2004).

Managerialism A central pillar of neoliberal thought was that private enterprise was good and public services were bad; the answer was to transfer managerial practices – rooted in competition and consumer choice – from the former to the latter. The impact of New Public Management (NPM) on policing was considerable (Leishman et al, 1996).

Privatisation A very influential development has been the expansion of the private sector in criminal justice. There are now large numbers of uniformed personnel working for private security companies, governments increasingly employ private security, as do some police forces, and private prisons have been introduced (first in the US and later in the UK). These developments indicate that the state is willing to contract out segments of the criminal justice system that were previously the monopoly of state agencies (Jones and Newburn, 1998; Stenning, 2000).

Technology The information, communication and technology (or ICT) revolution of the past two decades has had a tremendous impact on policing. Ericson and Haggerty (1997) argue that this has turned the police into 'knowledge brokers', feeding information into a number of systems. Computer and information technology has become central to policing.

Internationalisation Some forms of crime, including some new ones, have become increasingly international in scope and this has had a considerable impact on patterns of crime and cross-border policing. This has led to the establishment of an international criminal justice fraternity, fed by conferences and seminars, and an industry purveying law enforcement programmes and products (Brogden, 2005). Policing has responded with the creation of informal and formal structures and with agencies to cope with cross-border crime. Most prominent are Interpol and more recently Europol, but for many years the DEA (Drug Enforcement Agency of the US) has been active in a large number of countries including the Netherlands (Punch, 1985; Nadelman, 1993).

Partnerships and 'multilateralisation' From having a monopoly on fighting crime, the police organisation has moved to engage increasingly in multi-agency partnerships – with business corporations and other enterprises, private security companies, schools, social work agencies, mental heath services, community groups, and so on. Bayley and Shearing (2001) use the term 'multilateralisation' to convey the diverse levels of security provision that typify modern societies; they refer to this new nexus as the 'governance of security'.

Media and crime In the US and the UK in particular, the media has begun to highlight issues of crime and crime control with a populist 'law and order' slant that argues for tougher measures and heavier sanctions. This tends to focus on weaknesses in the criminal justice system, soft sentencing and ineffective policing (absence of policing from the streets and lax law enforcement), with an emphasis on the plight of the victims, the demonisation of serious criminals and out-groups, demands for tougher sanctions and new legislation.

Militarisation Some scholars have documented developments at the 'sharp end' of policing. Kraska (2001) in particular has revealed that in the US there has been an increase in specially trained and heavily equipped paramilitary units (often referred to as 'SWAT' squads). And in violent confrontations with demonstrators at major international gatherings in Seattle (1999), Genoa (2001) and Gothenburg (2001) the media conveyed the images of police in riot gear using tear gas and batons and brandishing weapons. In particular since the 9/11 terrorist attacks in the US, there has been an emphasis on strengthening security measures, with, on occasion, the visible presence of paramilitary units in a number of countries. There has also been enhanced cooperation between the military and the police.

Specialisation Increasingly, the police organisation has set up above the front-line, operational layer of patrol officers and detectives specialised units to cope with new forms of crime, ICT developments and new, scene-of-crime and DNA forensic techniques. More attention is given to victims – especially minors and victims of domestic and sexual violence – and new criminal areas such as hate crimes, cyber-crime, money-laundering, and so on. Policing has become more sophisticated, more technical and more skilled – and the expert is increasingly likely to be a civilian.

Economies of scale and national units In a number of countries, policing is primarily a local matter. This has often been conducted in relatively small units with strong community roots and with an aversion to national agencies. The past two decades have seen amalgamations of forces in several countries and/or regionalisation. Often this has been justified on the grounds of 'economies of scale'. New amalgamations were proposed in the UK and nationalisation in the Netherlands, although both initiatives have now been shelved. And governments are also pushing for national units to tackle serious crime across the country and across borders. This tendency was represented in a speech in London when the then Deputy Commissioner of the Met stated that there should be larger units in British policing and, to combat serious crime, there had to be expertise and operational capacity available at the national level (Blair, 2003).

Accountability A most significant factor in all this is that police officers have become more 'accountable' to governments, the courts, the press and the public for their policies and even for operational decisions. In several countries, there is ostensibly far more openness and transparency than ever before and senior officers are held to account on a number of fronts. There are concerns, however, about accountability in relation to new national units (on SOCA, the Serious Organised Crime Agency, see Bowling and Ross, 2006) and with regard to criminal justice institutions within the European Union (Loader, 2004).

Over the past two decades, these 12 key areas have combined to have a substantial impact on policy and practice in criminal justice in general and policing in particular. Added to this has been the rise of fundamental Muslim terrorism, with a series of high-casualty attacks across the globe, including 9/11 in the US and the London bomb attacks in 2005.

Police chiefs have had to learn to take account of these multiple, macro-developments alongside the daily tasks of running their organisations and balancing the books (one chief constable told me the first thing he asks about an incident is, 'What will it cost?'). British police chiefs were now seen as 'managers' in the light of NPM and were expected to achieve centrally set targets while delivering value for money. In particular, they were tasked to tackle crime 'robustly' or their organisations might be deemed not 'fit for purpose'. Unfortunately, reducing crime has proved to be a difficult task. A pivotal problem for the police is that they simply cannot seem to deliver on the one competency that is continually demanded of them – combating crime. Moreover, an over-emphasis on crime control distorts the broader police mandate and alienates citizens whose information, cooperation and trust is essential to the healthy and effective functioning of the police in a democratic society (Loveday, 1996, p 98). Bayley (1994) admirably summarises the research data on this with a strong emphasis on the US; more up-to-date overviews may be found in Waddington (1999), Newburn (2003, 2005) and Reiner (2006). It is important to recognise that the police by themselves cannot make substantial inroads on many forms of crime.

Victimisation studies show that much crime is not reported to the police and only a small proportion of crime is 'solved'. There is much evidence to indicate that the police are dependent on the support of the public to perform their tasks effectively and they will only gain that cooperation from citizens when they enjoy credibility and legitimacy among the public (Tyler and Huo, 2002). Furthermore, the police organisation is the only visible, uniformed agency that is accessible to the public 24 hours a day; it has always attracted demands for help and this led me in an earlier work to dub the police agency the 'secret social service' (Punch, 1979b).

In short, the police agency alone can only have a marginal impact on crime, yet it is often the single most important criterion on which police performance is judged. If police officers, politicians and others proclaim that crime control is the **core**

business of the police, they are burdening the organisation with an assignment that is difficult to fulfil and that threatens to distort its relationship with the public (an element in what Manning (1977) referred to as the 'impossible mandate' of policing).

This must be most frustrating for a (hypothetical) police chief returning from a session in the Himalayas on spiritual leadership where she also has pondered on corporate strategy, scenarios for policing Dorset in 2025, and a new digital mission statement, only to be besieged by a badgering Cabinet Office ("Number Ten on the line, ma'am"), surrounded by Home Office officials overreacting to every trifling incident, pursued by an increasingly impertinent and intrusive media and having to listen to armchair academics who assert that 'nothing works'! Moreover, despite the requirement for chief officers to achieve academically and prove their managerial skills, the profession has been subject to criticism in the media. In a portrait of chief constables and their qualifications in *The Daily Telegraph* (Johnston and Steele, 2000), for example, disparaging remarks are made about those with degrees in management or social sciences. The article reported that 'Bramshill puts the emphasis on corporate management skills rather than old-style thief-catching' (Bramshill educates senior police officers as part of Centrex, National Police Training). A remark by the programme director of the Strategic Command Course that the primary focus on the course was not crime management elicited the ire of the newspaper and the caustic headline, 'Chasing criminals? That's not their job'.

In a way, however, the newspaper was right: the British police elite had become not only distinctly managerial but also relatively liberal. It had become 'Scarmanised' after Lord Scarman's report on the Brixton riots, which essentially called for a return to 'policing by consent' and away from confrontation. Indeed, the spark that ignited the riots was a heavy-handed enforcement approach that now looks like a forerunner of zero tolerance tactics. Some of those chiefs had resented the crude way the police had been used by government in breaking the 1984 miners' strike. And the police elite had taken on board in recent years one of the managerial mantras that policing was a service that should be responsive to its 'customers'. Yet, when consulted, those customers rarely mentioned 'crime' and instead came up with an array of largely local, 'nuisance' issues related to feelings of insecurity, noisy neighbours, graffiti, vandalism, incivilities and dirt. Dog droppings began increasingly to land, as it were, on many a local commander's desk. Above all, communities wanted to see *local* police officers who were visible, available, competent, approachable and geared up to taking their problems seriously. In London, a survey by Fitzgerald et al (2002), *Policing for London*, or PFLS, indicated that people wanted a more visible and responsive police agency that was engaged with the local community. The majority wanted more police, but a different police: yet the broad thrust of the PFLS findings was that in 2000 Londoners found their police less responsive, less visible, less accessible and less engaged with the community than they would like. Last but not least, many chief officers had been exposed in seminars and degree programmes to the views of academics, and the evidence of research, that the police alone can only have a minor impact on many forms of crime.

However, having assiduously done their homework and having conscientiously endeavoured to change their spots to cope with multiple and not always consistent demands, they were now being accused of failing to be 'old-time thief-catchers'. Of great significance was the fact that both of the major political parties, with the popular press proving highly influential, had for some time turned to crime control as a prime electoral issue. In essence, many politicians and the tabloid newspapers took the position that the 'core business' of policing was **fighting crime** (and this was explicit in the Audit Commission report of 1993).

Indeed, in debates and policies on policing in a number of western societies, it is possible to observe periodic shifting, and even oscillation, between two main 'paradigms' (by paradigm is meant an institutional mind-set, or an explicit or implicit 'philosophy' of policing). Often these are framed or formally articulated when a new agency is set up or there is a substantial societal and/or institutional shift. We can trace one, for example, to the statements of Sir Robert Peel around the founding of the 'new police' in London in 1829 (Critchley, 1978). Another was articulated during the reform process in Northern Ireland when the Patten Commission (Patten Report, 1999) adopted a 'human rights' paradigm for future policing in the province. Yet another was shaped in South Africa by the move from the apartheid regime to democratic government and the creation of SAPS, the South African Police Service (Marks, 2005).

These competing philosophies are linked to contrasting views of the fundamental mandate of the police organisation. In the 'crime control' paradigm, the police apparatus is primarily geared to law enforcement and crime control as its central activity in a largely repressive style. This is sometimes referred to as the 'professional' model based on the 'three Rs' – random patrol, rapid response and reactive investigation (also known as 'get tough' and its proponents as 'lock 'em ups' – Lardner, 1997, p 55). In the 'consent and service' paradigm, in contrast, the emphasis is far more on 'root causes' and on a socially engaged agency with a broad service orientation, crime prevention, multi-agency cooperation and drawing on the concept of 'policing by consent' (Alderson, 1979). This broader scope is geared to the 'three Ps' of prevention, problem solving and partnership (Bratton, 1997).

It could be argued that the first paradigm is almost universally the 'predominant' one. For instance, the British police elite may have moved closer to the second paradigm, but there is a wealth of research that indicates that segments of the police organisation and the resilient occupational culture (the infamous 'canteen culture') remain fixated on 'catching crooks' and a crime control focus (Manning, 1997a). The predilection for a more assertive and robust policing style during the past few years in the Netherlands, for example, can be viewed as a periodic swing to the first model, with 'catching crooks' being bandied about by some top cops as their main priority. This would have been treated with withering derision a decade earlier.

Furthermore, our beleaguered chiefs found that not only Conservative governments but also New Labour, in office from 1997, insistently demanded crime reduction from the police. A response to this external pressure, continual turbulence and escalating expectations was for some to opt for an accent on change, for tough talk and for swiftly taking on ideas and practices from 'flagship' forces elsewhere in order to project an aura of forceful innovation. In an examination of the Dutch policing elite (Boin et al, 2003), for instance, we can observe motivated and industrious leaders energetically reorganising their forces. Indeed, according to one police researcher I interviewed for the project on zero tolerance, "there is an unbridled urge to innovate … people are tripping over one another with every sort of innovation and all sorts of initiatives". The police chiefs, he continued, also engage in a form of 'concept consumerism', whereby they swiftly adopt new terms or metaphors from foreign fads and fashions, spraying English buzz-words and phrases such as 'reassurance', 'broken windows', 'quality of life', 'intelligence-led' and so on throughout their interviews. Concepts such as 'inverted pyramid', 'active prevention', 'core tasks', 'quality systems' and 'the police as a production company' are bandied about, while the 'new hype,' according to van der Vijver (2004, p 102), is inventing a domestic (and almost untranslatable) vocabulary for 'different sorts of police such as Proximity Police, Control Police, etc'.

In this respect, police chiefs have started to behave no differently than managers in business, who, after all, have been continually held up as role models for the public services. It is somewhat ironic, then, that an examination of business literature and managerial practice reveals a predilection for the superficial and for slavishly picking up any new, trendy idea or concept. In this context, it debatable to what extent the best-selling text *Who Moved My Cheese?* with over 20 million copies sold (Johnson, 1998), is a guideline for conduct in the real world: some commentators were critical of its homilies and, more generally, the editor of *The Economist* dismissed much managerial advice from gurus as '99% bullshit' (Knights and McCabe, 2003, p 46). For it remains the case – despite a multitude of prestigious business schools, a vast management literature, an army of gurus and cohorts of consultants – that no one can say precisely which organisational model works best and which specific policy will guarantee success. *In Search of Excellence*, by Peters and Waterman (1982), for instance, sold more than 12 million copies worldwide, but over half of the 'excellent' companies portrayed in it were in deeply troubled water within five years of publication. A few years ago, Enron and WorldCom were leading companies, attracting plaudits for their exemplary performance, whereas now some of their executives are facing long jail sentences and Enron has gone out of business. This constant uncertainty in management, some argue, generates considerable neuroticism about seeking success and about 'what works' (Knights and McCabe, 2003). Displaying no neurotic doubts, the rapacious John Paul Getty replied in old age to a question about the key to his success: "Get up early, work hard and find oil"!

Doubtless contemporary police chiefs get up early and work hard: but where do they find oil? In the mid-1990s, it was asserted that 'oil' was gushing from the pavements of Manhattan. A mayor and police chief in New York had, it seemed, developed a brand new policing policy called 'zero tolerance'. This, it was claimed, had brought down the crime figures in the 'Big Apple' dramatically. This appeared to be what everyone was looking for because large American cities had been notoriously crime-ridden and, if a means for reducing crime had been discovered, it must be highly promising. Within a short period, droves of police officers, prosecutors, judges, civic officials, mayors and politicians began flocking to New York. These included delegations from the UK and the Netherlands.

The punitive element in the American criminal justice system, however, was miles away from the enlightened and tolerant views on crime and punishment in the Netherlands. Why, then, did Dutch police officers, politicians and other officials pay so much attention in the middle of the nineties to the hard 'zero tolerance policing' of the US? New York still exerts a strong attraction: a 25-person delegation from Amsterdam visited the city in 2004. The leader of the Labour Party on the city council was clearly impressed with New York's record: "Thanks to zero tolerance all the crime figures in New York have dropped dramatically" (Beusekamp, 2004, p 3). Apart from the fact that this was quite inaccurate, the irony was that the Labour Party in Amsterdam was not only long considered the progressive bulwark of 'red' ideology and practice, but also had typically displayed an innate distrust of the police and anything smacking of authority. The Dutch Left, following Britain with Blair and New Labour as its model, had discovered law and order – and soundbites.

These developments raise one's curiosity as to which interpretative lenses policy makers, police officers and others employ when scrutinising concepts and practices from outside, what 'filters' are used to select practices and later, if these are subsequently implemented within institutions, what adaptations are made. Although I have emphasised the fact that the police in Britain have faced unprecedented pressure to change in recent years, and there are chief officers who firmly pronounce that they are ready for change (Blair, 2003), there is general pessimism in the literature about the willingness and ability of the police organisation and culture to change substantially (Chan, 1997). In the US, for instance, a book on police accountability reports that: 'The history of police reform is filled with stories of highly publicized changes that promised much but evaporated over the long run with only minimal impact', and that 'Many cynics believe that the American police are incapable of reforming themselves and that the police subculture is resistant to all efforts to achieve accountability' (Walker, 2005, p 17).

A few years ago, a British police chief spoke about introducing 'problem-oriented policing' in her force: 'This is something we picked up from the United States. It was very successfully tried out over there in San Diego' (Clare, 1998, p 9). This is despite the fact that 'problem-oriented policing' (or POP) dates from at least 20 years earlier (Goldstein, 1979) and had been adopted in many forces in many countries including the UK. There was even an overview from the Home Office available at the time, detailing the British experience with POP (Leigh et al, 1996). It claimèd that POP was never seriously implemented, was used as a label for short-term, limited campaigns and was generally poorly managed with limited resource leading to the early abandonment of POP projects. But how is it possible that she can boldly refer to POP as something *new*?

Is it that police chiefs, and politicians, suffer from a form of conceptual myopia and institutional amnesia that (conveniently) allows them to forget the past and recycle old concepts as new? 'Neighbourhood-oriented policing' (NOP), for example, has recently resurfaced in government policy, although one chief officer that I interviewed in 2006 said that "this is the fourth time I've been through this cycle". Then, reflecting on a project on diversity within the Greater Manchester Police that commenced with much promise but soon 'evaporated' with loss of staff and purpose, its director states: "One aspect of [police] culture, often neglected in the literature, is the endemic 'short-termist' approach in the service which leads to organisational 'memory loss'.... This explains why the police so often seem to revisit issues in cyclical fashion" (cited in Waddington, 2007).

It would be easy to be sceptical, too, about a visit to Chicago in 2005 by the Dutch Minister of the Interior with several leading mayors to look at policing and safety. The subsequent report on television followed several Chicago police officers engaged in identical activities to those that Dutch officers have been deeply involved in for some 20 years. This revealed the dramaturgy of politics, whereby officials wish to show that they are at the cutting edge of international developments and return from (expensive) trips abroad with a 'new' conceptual vocabulary that is, in reality, old wine.

In turning, then, to the adoption by the British and Dutch police of concepts and practices from the US and, in particular, so-called zero tolerance policing, the focus will be on **policy transfer** in policing. In the academic literature on transfer in criminal justice, there are two main perspectives. The first emphasises convergence through structural developments in the post-modern, global society: it suggests a growing consensus in criminal justice matters, with the US as the prime motor, and that western democracies are following a similar path. This is something of a 'McDonaldisation' thesis (Ritzer, 1997), that in criminal justice, powerful political and commercial interests are promoting change globally (through a 'prison-industrial complex'; Christie, 2000). Indeed, at a conference in London in 2004, a British police chief remarked, "If we haven't been to America, then apparently we're not much good". This does assume that there is some distinctly 'American' criminal justice export article when, in fact, America is very diverse, with no single model of policy and practice and no single driver of policy. Generally, reform of the police in the US is fundamentally local, whereas in Europe the central state is the key actor (Bayley, 2006).

The second perspective is based on complexity and diversity and that 'political agency' – that is, the role and influence of gatekeepers, policy makers, and even warring factions within criminal justice – means that outcomes are defined by debate and disputes among these diverse figures. There is no determinism that a specific model will be adopted as that depends on a variety of contingent variables within a specific political context and a particular policy arena. It may be the case that both perspectives are valid to a certain extent; that there is a growing consensus in criminal justice, but that political and other elites in individual countries continue to 'filter' policies to adapt them to local needs and views.

This work takes the second standpoint as its primary accent, with the focus on the processes of policy transfer in two countries, drawing on a book by Newburn and Sparks (2004). They raise a number of key questions culminating in 'How complete is the process?' and 'How is the process related to policy "success" or "failure"'? They argue, for example, that in the UK there was no simple transfer of US policy into policing; they examine this view in relation to three areas in criminal justice, of which one is zero tolerance. Tonry (2004), however, does argue that much of the punitive rhetoric in American criminal justice was copied by British politicians and the media, and that this did influence to a certain degree legislation, policy and practice (as in the 1998 Crime and Disorder Act and the 2003 Anti-Social Behaviour Act).

With regard to the Netherlands, moreover, policing and criminal justice may appear to be effectively nationally organised. Surely in this ostensibly homogenous society, there must be a high measure of consensus on policy and practice and this must be an ideal environment for innovation because the system is relatively small and coherent and can be steered from the centre? But in my 30 years experience of involvement with the Dutch police, I have observed and encountered much local chauvinism, an insistence on the regional context, resistance to central control ('them in The Hague'), and resentment of the dominance of the '*Randstad*' (the western part of the country with the four major cities) and of the 'arrogance' of the Amsterdam police, the lead force. When I travelled to the 'deep south' or 'high north' of the country, never more than two hours by train, I often encountered a frosty reception when lecturing on corruption in Amsterdam: the attitude was that such things simply did not happen in their province and some officers spoke of the *Randstad* almost as a foreign country. For some Dutch forces it seemed easier to transfer an innovation from Edmonton than from Amsterdam! The attitude 'Interesting, but not invented here' is not unknown in policing, especially when it stems from the lead force (and see the reaction above to Maples trying to 'sell' the New York model in New Orleans). Dixon and Maher (2004, p 261) note a similar ambivalence in Australian policing, with a syndrome of outer deference to ideas from the UK and US – a 'cultural cringe that overvalues almost anything from overseas' – coupled with 'resistance to following either the old or the new imperial master's lead'. In South Africa, which has witnessed an invasion of expertise from abroad to help reform the police since the end of *apartheid*, one officer reacted to the attempt to introduce a human rights dimension with "don't try to push this constitution down my throat" (Hornberger, 2007). Almost paradoxically, then, multilingual Dutch officers assiduously travel the world but remain in many respects highly parochial: these 'frequent flyer cops' talk global but act local.

This duality is doubtless related to the nature of much day-to-day policing, which is strongly rooted historically and operationally in specific localities and territories (Waddington, 1999). Interpreting such obstacles, resistance and hiccups around innovation depends also on one's perspective on organisations and systems. It is possible to make a global or macro-analysis at the system level, but one can also – departing more from an interactionist or critical theoretical view – maintain that organisations are intricate, complex and fluctuating entities where reality is constantly being redefined (Rock, 1978). One's interpretation of developments in policing depends on which lens one uses to view 'reality' and I am particularly mindful of the negotiated nature and complexity of the processes in reform and innovation in policing.

The following chapters look at the influence of New York and its model of 'zero tolerance', and, in scrutinising what happened in the UK and the Netherlands with respect to the introduction of this 'new' style of policing, raise the following questions:

* What is zero tolerance – particularly its New York variant – and why did it prove so attractive to police forces abroad?
* How did it transfer to the UK and the Netherlands? These are two valuable and contrasting case studies. In the UK it might be assumed that zero tolerance would find fertile ground in policing, given the political and press support for crime control. In contrast, the Netherlands may seem to represent the antipathy of such an approach, given that country's long adhesion to an alternative style of criminal justice (much closer to the 'service' paradigm). How, then, do policies 'travel' and what 'filters' are employed in the process of transfer?
* Finally, what does this tell us about the current state of policing and about shifting paradigms?

The New York 'miracle'

2

I n the early 1990s, the US was enjoying economic prosperity, but there were two things blighting the most powerful and wealthy country in the world.

First, urban America was afflicted by serious and violent crime and there was widespread fear of crime. The cover of *Time* magazine on 23 August 1993 read 'America the violent: crime is spreading and patience is running out' (Smolowe, 1993). *Business Week* (13 December 1993) wrote on 'The economics of crime: the toll is frightening; can anything be done?', and estimated the country's total annual expenditure on crime to be some $90 billion. It is tempting with hindsight to see this as a turning point in political and public determination to 'do something' about crime.

Second, the deprivation in parts of American cities was appalling. Poverty and discrimination had been reported in detail by academics and journalists for several decades, but by now the contrast between 'private affluence and public squalor' in American society was stark. Conditions in the ghettos sometimes approached those of developing countries. This was illustrated by an image on the cover of *The Economist* (6 November 1993), which displayed an elderly black man, walking bowed with the aid of a stick, along a dilapidated street that looked like a war zone. The caption was 'Hell is an American city'.

Crime and urban blight were spoiling the American success story. In New York, however, things were about to change.

The New York story, a kind of criminological 'miracle' that drew many pilgrims to worship at Police Plaza in downtown Manhattan, has its roots in three main factors:

* Crime and disorder were seriously affecting economic life and the reputation of the city; the centre of global capitalism was unsafe and violent.
* The election of Giuliani as mayor brought in a highly ambitious political figure with a determination to leave his mark on the city. His campaign message was 'it is disorder that is driving the city down'.
* Giuliani found in William Bratton a police chief who had a record of bringing down crime levels in the subway system and who also appeared to possess the ability to reorganise the city police force.

Together Giuliani and Bratton were determined to tackle New York's crime problem. Initially, the approach attracted the label 'zero tolerance policing' from politicians and the media. The expression had entered political parlance in the

1980s as a term for resolute, unbending policy. Then, in a number of campaigns, citizen groups demanded 'zero tolerance' enforcement of specific offences in the face of alleged 'slack' police enforcement. For instance, Mothers Against Drunk Driving (MADD) maintained that driving under the influence of alcohol among youths, a major cause of serious and fatal road accidents, was being 'under-policed' and should be dealt with through a universal policy of remorseless enforcement. In response to this campaign, President Clinton spoke in 1995 of 'zero tolerance laws' with regard to drunk driving by minors. Giuliani also used the term in his electoral campaign for Mayor of New York in 1994 (Karmen, 2004).

So what were Bratton's strategy and methods with regard to policing? This is best approached by a four-pronged examination of the New York experience:

- Bratton and the subway system;
- Bratton and the New York City Police Department (NYPD);
- 'Fixing broken windows';
- What is 'zero tolerance policing' or ZTP? And why did it prove so attractive to the many criminal justice 'pilgrims' who flocked in their hundreds to New York?

Bratton and the subway system

Many of the ideas and techniques later used by Bratton with the NYPD were developed earlier when he took charge of the New York City Transit Police Department, which was responsible for policing the extensive subway and surface rail system (used by some three and half million people daily). He was assisted there by Jack Maple, who had become impressed with the value of using crime data. Maple later moved with Bratton to the NYPD and helped to set up 'Compstat' (see p 16):

> He [Maple] told anyone who would listen that until the entire police force got out of its rut – until police officers got out of their patrol cars and started *fighting crime* instead of responding to 911 calls – until that happened, the crime rate would keep climbing. Maple started mapping strategies to fight crime, and papered his walls with fifty-five feet of hand-drawn maps he called Charts of the Future. The charts detailed every stop on every subway line and every robbery that had been committed. The idea was obvious but untested: go after the bad guys where the bad guys did their work and get them before they committed more crimes. (Remnick, 1997, p 96)

The subway system runs continually and the trains and stations had become the haven of 'street people'. (The expression 'street people' is meant here as a neutral term to describe people who live and function on the street. It does not imply that these people are criminal or even necessarily 'disorderly'; indeed, it is recognised that the poor, homeless, sick and disadvantaged who end up on the street are often the victims of crime.) The fact that street people could ride the subway trains continually, and could inhabit the stations at night, meant that many passengers felt unsafe on the subway and many people avoided travelling on the subway altogether. This had serious financial consequences, both for the railway company in terms of loss of fares, and for businesses in the city in terms of poor accessibility for personnel and clients.

Bratton attacked the problem in a forceful manner that was soon to become familiar:

*   many more uniformed officers than before were sent out on patrol duty;
*   stations were made physically safer by blocking off opportunities for crime and for sleeping; unmanned stations were given station managers who reclaimed 'ownership' of their territory;
*   the law was consistently and persistently enforced in areas such as fare dodging, sleeping in stations, begging, using the trains as a refuge, defecating and urinating in public places, writing graffiti, behaving in a drunk and disorderly manner and, in particular, threatening other passengers;
*   more effort was put into documenting enforcement measures, with statistics that soon detailed a dramatic drop in crime on the subway system.

Bratton claimed that enforcement against relatively minor offences and 'disorderly behaviour' often led to arrests for more serious offences and/or to information that aided in solving other crimes; somehow fare dodging, disorder and robbery were all perceived to be one problem, 'one seamless web' (Kelling and Coles, 1996).

Bratton was, in effect, using intensive patrolling, persistent enforcement pressure, situational crime control and rapid analysis of information. These became his trademarks. The subway example conveyed the message that, as a result of Bratton's actions, the transport system was cleaner and safer, that New Yorkers could use it with little fear and that it was economically more efficient. The icing on the cake, however, was that the crime rate had, according to Bratton, been significantly reduced (Bratton and Knobler, 1998).

Bratton and the NYPD

Bratton's success did not escape the attention of Mayor Giuliani, who recruited him from Boston where he had become Police Commissioner, to head the NYPD in 1994. The NYPD is the largest police department in the US, with around 28,000 officers in 1994 (currently, it has almost 40,000 officers). It also has a history of periodic corruption, the latest scandal being in 1994 (Mollen Commission, 1994). In fact Bowling (1999, p 538) maintains that in the late 1980s 'police morale, motivation and activity were at an all-time low' and that the NYPD was 'characterised as passive and cautious to the point that all that mattered was "cover your back"'. It was this highly criticised and demoralised force that Bratton revitalised within two years; he also put the NYPD on the international map for something other than corruption. How did he go about it?

First, the NYPD put many more uniformed personnel out on the streets and recruited 6,000 new officers. With the amalgamation of several other smaller forces, including the Transit Police, and with officers in the pipeline from federal funding, this eventually brought the numbers of officers to nearly 40,000. This greatly increased the visibility of the police in the eyes of the public.

The major thrust of patrolling was to curb the aggressive and disorderly behaviour of street people, such as begging, sleeping rough and committing petty crime. 'Squeegee men', who cleaned car windows at traffic lights and then forcefully demanded a tip, were a particular target; they figured prominently in Giuliani's mayoral campaign. In the new rhetoric that was adopted, these were dubbed 'quality of life' offences; but again, as in the subway, the claim was made that enforcement against relatively minor offences and 'disorderly behaviour' often led to arrests for more serious offences and helped solve other crimes (Kelling and Coles, 1996, p 142). Indeed, there were data to support a dramatic drop in crime in the city, including serious and violent crime.

Another of Bratton's tactics was to improve quality of life and enhance the economic climate by 'reclaiming' parts of the city (railway stations, parks and areas around public buildings). This was stimulated by creating partnerships between businesses, private security and the police in areas known as Business Improvement Districts (BIDs). These initiatives were largely financed by private funding. Bratton spoke of 'taking back the city, street by street, block by block' (Silverman, 1999, p 90). Bryant Park, which had been taken over by drug addicts and sex workers who left used condoms and needles in their debris, was 'reclaimed' by 'disbanding' the various groups that had taken it over for their own use to the extent that locals had avoided it. By improving security, lighting and rest rooms, and installing flowerbeds, kiosks for food and drink, clearly posted rules and private security patrols allied to the police, the park became attractive once more to residents (Kelling and Coles, 1996). The same process of 'gentrification' took place elsewhere, including Grand Central Station and around the New York Public Library.

A significant tool in galvanising the force into action was 'Compstat.' This started as a computer programme to analyze crime data but this became the basis of a 'strategic control system'(Weisburd et al, 2005, p 511). This had two main components. First, Bratton **demanded good and timely information on crime patterns**; and second, he **called precinct commanders to account**. At Compstat meetings at headquarters, precinct commanders would be confronted with data on crime patterns using 'digital mapping', questioned on their policies with regard to 'hot spots' and put under pressure to perform and to 'hit the numbers' (Loveday and Reid, 2003). Sherman, a leading criminologist, called this unprecedented, that in New York and US policing 'top police executives pay attention to street-level crime. Most chiefs are caught up with managing the hospital rather than worrying about diseases. Crime is left to the soldiers, and the generals pay no attention' (Montgomery, 1997, p 3).

There was an abrasive 'kicking butt' element to these confrontations and some officers were even dismissed for performing poorly at meetings. Maple often chaired the Compstat sessions, and he did so with 'humor, swagger, praise, or insult, depending on what was necessary'. On one occasion, for example, when a chief 'seemed to be fudging his way through a report, Maple projected a picture of Pinocchio on the wall' (Remnick, 1997, p 97)

This at times abrasive, 'in your face,' confrontational style with senior officers in the presence of outsiders may be socially acceptable in New York and elsewhere in the US; it is certainly part of the assertive, macho-style management prevalent in a number of American companies. Whether this confrontational style can be culturally transplanted to other societies with quite different styles of interaction among senior professionals is an interesting question.

Two other factors were at play in New York. First, the commanders were offered operational support and tactical advice from the centre; it was not all bullying and confrontation. And, second, the meetings were open to invited spectators, from 'Australia to Zimbabwe', and there could be as many as 140 people in the room (Peters, 2004). Politicians, policy makers, judges, mayors, academics and police chiefs from many countries from around the world witnessed the 'miracle' at work (Silverman, 1999, p 123).

'Fixing broken windows'

> Maple said to me, 'Don't tell the Commish [Police Commissioner Bratton], but I never bothered to read "Broken windows". Shoot me.' (Remnick, 1997, p 100)

George Kelling and J.Q. Wilson had written an article on 'Broken windows' in 1982. The argument was that areas with a symbol of decay — one 'broken window'— are likely to enter a cycle of dilapidation, with more destruction of property and with the respectable inhabitants fleeing the area (Wilson and Kelling, 1982). The answer, then, was to reclaim the area though a multi-agency approach that fixed the 'broken windows' by attending to the physical environment, but also by providing a feeling of security with visible control agents. The argument was that you fixed the problems, reversed the decline and reclaimed the community. Bowling (1996) views this broken windows 'theory' as no more than a suggestive metaphor based on a dubious experiment. Others were also critical (Manning, 1997b), but the concept was most influential in the thinking of Bratton and others (Montgomery, 1997, p 2). The NYPD approach incorporated some of the ideas derived from Wilson and Kelling, but it became associated with the term 'zero tolerance'. Bratton himself stopped using this catch phrase (he had employed it initially in the context of combating corruption). One of his advisers in New York was George Kelling: when Kelling came to the Netherlands in 1998 to lecture on what was advertised as 'zero tolerance,' his opening line was that he was not going to talk about zero tolerance!

One of the reasons for this appears to have been that zero tolerance policing, or 'ZTP', was misappropriated to justify crude 'sweeping' operations – known as 'Weed and Seed', 'Clean Sweep' and 'Operation CLEAN' – where street people were virtually run out of town or out of certain areas. In some American cities – including Baltimore, San Francisco and Seattle – civil rights groups mounted legal action against ZTP, sometimes successfully (Kelling and Coles, 1996). In fairness, both Bratton and Kelling maintained that there was far more to ZTP than 'cracking down' on street people.

In *Fixing Broken Windows*, Kelling and Coles (1996) endeavour to explain what that 'more' consists of. In essence, they argue strongly for adopting new forms of community-oriented policing (COP) and problem-oriented policing (POP). They draw their inspiration from impeccable sources: from Sir Robert Peel (founding father of the Metropolitan Police in 1829), Egon Bittner (pioneering sociologist of the police) and Herman Goldstein (who first formulated POP and was something of a mentor to Kelling). In short, Kelling, in his book with Coles, distances himself from hard-line policing and propagates 'a new paradigm' of COP based on an active citizenry, a new communitarianism and a concerted, multi-agency approach to tackling disorder, enhancing the quality of life, restoring security and reducing fear of crime (Kelling and Coles, 1996, p 1).

But Bowling (1996) argues persuasively that Kelling, Wilson and others who propagated broken windows were also simultaneously advocating aggressive order maintenance patrolling. There were three main difficulties with what was fundamentally a plea to combine 'soft' and 'hard' policing in a holistic policy for community renewal.

First, it relied on treacly jargon that was hard to define and the broken windows metaphor is highly debatable: who defined quality of life, what was 'disorder' and what did it mean to 'take back' a community – and at whose expense? There was dangerous ambivalence in these mixed messages:

> The notion of 'fixing broken windows' elaborated in Wilson's and Kelling's papers on order maintenance can be interpreted as a euphemism for 'fixing' those people seen as 'disreputable' through the use of aggressive policing. The imagery turns an eyesore, or a lone prostitute, into menace and danger and street people are conveyed as surly and aggressive. Their main policy recommendation to the police is to 'kick ass'. However, aggressive enforcement does not hold out the possibility of repair of communities ravaged by poverty, drug abuse, widespread availability of firearms and the entrenchment of violence. Rather, it represents a superficial palliative to a set of fundamental social problems which are, at best, unaffected by police strategies and, at worst, exacerbated by them. (Bowling, 1999, p 548)

Broken windows and zero tolerance could easily lead to intolerance, exclusion and demonisation of out-groups, according to critics.

Second, could the police, by taking the lead, breathe life into defunct 'communities'? Did they have the pulling and staying power and were they not perhaps chasing a nostalgic notion of community?

Third, and most crucially, many observers simply assumed that the central message was that ZTP, seen as aggressive patrol against 'disorder', could reduce crime. The criminal justice 'tourists' took back the simplistic message that it could also work for them, for Bratton's message was 'if you can make it in New York you can make it anywhere' (Dixon, 2005, p 485). ZTP was the universal castor oil for cutting crime.

Why did ZTP appear so attractive?

Bratton and Giuliani had apparently, then, 'reduced crime', and they had undoubtedly made New York a safer and more pleasant city. This attracted attention from all over the world. Bratton's portrait appeared on the cover of *Time* magazine in 1996. This was enough, however, for the ambitious Giuliani apparently to squeeze him out for taking all the glory for *his* policies. Bratton then became a consultant to other forces and, like Kelling and later Giuliani, travelled the globe as a criminal justice guru, selling his message on 're-engineering' policing (he is currently Chief of the Los Angeles Police Department). This took him to Rio de Janeiro (one wonders what he achieved there with its incredibly high levels of crime and police violence; Hinton, 2006), to Australia, where he was hailed as the 'the man to fix Sydney' (Dixon and Maher, 2004, p 255), and to Hartlepool.

But of key significance is the overriding issue of whether the NYPD had 'really' reduced crime? Academics and others scrutinised the evidence and argued that crime was already falling in New York before the introduction of ZTP and that this phenomenon could also be witnessed in cities that did not propagate ZTP (Karmen, 2001). In San Diego, using largely a community-oriented approach that was the antipathy of ZTP, crime also dropped (Greene, 1999). Indeed, crime was also falling in many other societies (Tonry, 2004). Of course, the new-style police approach must have had an impact on certain offences in certain locations, but the fall in crime was clearly caused by a serendipitous constellation of variables.

It was also argued by critics and parts of the media that the assertiveness of ZTP could turn into aggression, and there were examples of excess violence, notably in the Louima and Diallo cases (Smith, 2004, p 202). The officers who seriously abused Louima said to him, "This is Giuliani time"; and the officers who fired 41 shots at Diallo, hitting him 19 times, were part of a new, elite, aggressive, plain-clothes 'Street Crime Unit', focusing on serious street crime as part of the ZTP campaign (Karmen, 2004, p 31). There was even talk of 'broken heads':

> This Broken Window theory can quickly deteriorate into the Broken Head theory ... 'making all these arrests is going to give a large number of arrests to a large

number of people. So you make people less employable. And that is going to come back to haunt you'. (Montgomery, 1997, p 4)

There was, too, 'a steep and alarming rise in citizen complaints about abuse of authority, discourtesy, use of obscene language, and other infractions that indicate a brazen force' (Remnick, 1997, p 108).

What, then, was it that popularly became known as ZTP? It implied relentless attention to offences with no discretion, and that it was socially unacceptable that certain offences were not getting the attention they deserved. In popular discourse, it conveyed a new policy of tough enforcement of all offences, constant police pressure with high visibility and minimal discretion for officers on the street.

The catch phrase was applied to New York but what did it mean when translated in terms of policy and operational practice? In the NYPD 'model', we can discern a number of clear components:

- more uniformed and plain-clothes officers out on the streets;
- reclaiming public spaces;
- vigorously tackling 'disorder' and focusing on minor offences;
- keeping up the pressure with consistent and persistent enforcement;
- follow-up on warrants or non-compliance with arrests and prosecution;
- swift analysis and use of information;
- 'crime mapping' and targeting of 'hot spots' as well as hounding frequent offenders;
- pressuring senior officers to perform, with relentless follow-up on results and with the threat of career consequences;
- mobilising financial and other support from private enterprise;
- multi-agency cooperation;
- problem solving;
- community involvement;
- forceful leadership;
- advertising success.

This is obviously far more complex than some blanket assertion that no crime will be tolerated (which can never be fully implemented anyway), but it could be seen as precisely that by hard-liners. In effect, what Bratton and his staff had done was to come up with a formula that ostensibly combined COP and POP with modern information technology and aggressive patrol. Bratton then conducted himself like the charismatic, 'turn-around' manager of a large corporation: he identified himself with Iacocca, who had turned around Chrysler and his 'transformation' of the NYPD became a business school case. But, above all, he continued to hammer away at reducing crime; and the figures were all-important.

In the managerial jargon of the time, ZTP at the NYPD was dressed up as a paradigm shift of 're-engineering', although it is possible to discern in it a mishmash of COP, POP, ICT / Information and Communication Technology, broken windows, situational crime control, old-fashioned management by objectives and even an element of scientific management, viewing the lower ranks as servile assembly-line workers (Tilley, 2003; Dixon, 2005; Moore, 2005; Weisburd et al, 2005). Compstat won awards, was adopted in other forces and 'emerged as the NYPD's most permanent, far-reaching, and widely imitated innovation', according to Silverman (1999, p 124). Others are more sceptical and even call it 'archaic', while pointing out that similar systems were being developed elsewhere in the US prior to the New York model. It was also not particularly sophisticated and its inventors simply bought the software for the original computer programme at local stores (Weisburd et al, 2005).

Bratton also exemplified the police chief who gets out from behind the desk to motivate the troops, inspiring them at the same time as threatening to 'kick butt' for non-performance. Perhaps it is this ability to inspire, threaten and achieve results through 'transformational' leadership that has proved as influential as the label ZTP itself. For Bratton represented a new assertiveness, whereby police began to use intelligence-led policing, tackle crime by taking back public spaces, and concentrate on the offences and disorder that bother many people. This policy proved widely popular among many New York citizens and also became a major export article.

One feature of ZTP that did not travel well was the argument that focusing on disorder and minor crimes leads to the solving of more serious crimes. This does not appear to be universal and may be tied to the size and particular nature of the street population in the US. ZTP also runs the danger of encouraging aggressive policing against those who do not fit in.

Another important feature of the NYPD story, moreover, is that many American police chiefs serve at the whim of the mayor (the average tenure for a chief is roughly two years; Loveday and Reid, 2003). In 1999, for example, Baltimore elected a Republican, 'law and order' mayor. The police chief had originally been brought in to implement COP, but the mayor sacked him at their first meeting. When his deputy stood and 'and promised to push a "zero tolerance" strategy that the mayor found more appealing', he was promoted to chief of police on the spot (Skogan, 2006, p 9). Policy is primarily dictated by the local, elected politician – and every town is different. In the end, the key factor behind New York's success was Giuliani's burning ambition that fed his moral crusade to 'clean up' the city (Jones and Newburn, 2007).

My interpretation is that what foreign officials and police officers primarily took away from New York was the unequivocal message that, after years of being told 'nothing works', here was a positive innovation, a gleaming success story, to bring back home. However, Bowling makes the salient point that this was not so much 'new', but was more a restatement of a long-held, common-sense tradition in US policing in favour of aggressive enforcement against crime (1999, p 544). This is also the view of Manning (1997b, p 10), that American law enforcement periodically returns to 'real policing' with a tough public presence; he views ZTP as 'profoundly conservative and counterproductive'. What was new were the slogans shaped by the marketing techniques of merchandising and 'rebranding' (Silverman, 1999, p 88).

But there was also forceful, old-time martial imagery familiar from business battles and previous criminal justice campaigns, such as 'the war on drugs'. Here are some examples of the graphic imagery used in New York (emphasis added):

*   'NYPD *Battles Crime*' (the title of Silverman's (1999) somewhat uncritical book on the NYPD turnaround);
*   "We are doing something that to my knowledge has never been done before. We are fighting *the war on crime* as if it were really a *war*" (Maple, Bratton's right-hand man, cited in Andrews, 1997);
*   Bratton himself said of Operation Juggernaut (a crackdown on drug dealing): 'Prior to Juggernaut, the city's war on drugs had been our *Vietnam*: we were fighting a *hit-and-run enemy* and had gone in and made a lot of contact when we could, but we couldn't hold the ground. We didn't have the tactics or the *will to win*. Juggernaut was *the Normandy invasion*. We were going to *overwhelm our opponents*, take the ground and never leave, and systematically take them out…. We would *systematically take out* the low-level street dealer, the mid-level operator, and the high-level kingpin. *We would attack them* consistently on all fronts at all times. If you were a drug dealer, you were a *marked man*.' (Bratton with Knobler, 1998, p 275)

The metaphors may have been mixed, but the message was crystal clear and was further conveyed by the immodest title of Bratton's book, *Turnaround: How America's Top Cop Reversed the Crime Epidemic* (1998). After years of rising crime at an appalling cost, Bratton had apparently turned water into wine and had 'won' the war against crime in New York. The inference to be drawn by other police officers was that Bratton's NYPD had taken on the criminals and reduced crime: 'the department marketed a message; crime would be reduced substantially through assertive policing' (Silverman, 1999, p 88). They heard what they doubtless wanted to hear in simplistic slogans – such as 'the root cause of crime is the criminal' – and Bratton had apparently resolved the 'hard–soft' dichotomy by marrying COP, through 'broken windows', to being hard on crime. With new rhetoric and a new élan, the police could go out there, get back to 'real' police work, 'kick ass' and, above all, make a difference to the city. Furthermore, much of the public applauded the police for doing well after years of criticising them for underperforming and distrusting them because of corruption. Typically, Bratton coined an ironic one-liner: 'Crime is down in New York City: blame the police' (1997).

Zero tolerance policing: UK and the Netherlands

3

On 6 January 1997, Tony Blair, then Prime Minister-in-Waiting, was asked whether he agreed with 'so-called Zero-Tolerance policies – practised in New York and being experimented with in London's King's Cross – in which every law is clamped down on hard by police'. His affirmative answer, 'Yes I do' married New Labour to zero tolerance. The romance between the Labour party and 'New York style policing' began in the summer of 1995 when Shadow Home Secretary Jack Straw visited New York to meet police Commissioner William Bratton and his deputy Jack Maple. (Bowling, 1999, p 531)

Transfer to the UK

Of considerable interest is the path that ZTP took in the UK when it crossed the Atlantic. The UK appeared to be the western European state closest to the US in relation to 'toughness' in criminal justice, and the natural ally in the UK was the Conservative Party. Originally under Margaret Thatcher and from 1979 onwards, it had played the 'law and order' card. Conservative views were later typified by the statement in 1997, by the then Home Secretary Michael Howard, that 'prison works'. Howard was suggesting that the threat of long sentences for serious crime has a deterrent effect; informed opinion would not support this and would certainly not support the view that 'prison works'. But such populist and ideologically drenched soundbites that ignore the evidence but have wide populist appeal reflect the 'no-nonsense' tone of the debate in Britain (Downes and Morgan, 1997).

'Law and order' became a staple of political party debate from the 1979 election onwards, with increasing media attention while the Conservatives endeavoured to pillory Labour for being 'soft' on crime. In the 1990s, this led to an 'anything you can do, I can do tougher' stance, with law and order politics becoming 'a dominant discourse of the age: the "culture of control"' (Reiner, 2006, p 133). The Labour Party in opposition wanted to rid itself of that 'soft', liberal image. In 1996, Shadow Home Secretary Jack Straw launched a blistering attack on the Home Office and spoke of the 'crisis overwhelming the criminal justice system'. He maintained that more crimes were being committed and more people 'are getting away with it … we have to ensure more offenders are caught and convicted' (Rose, 2006). Labour had brazenly stolen the Conservatives' clothes while they were swimming. The new Labour leadership had taken its cue from President Clinton, a Democrat with progressive policies who had learned to lean to the right on key issues, including law and order. One of his pronouncements was reputed to be "never let the right get to the right of you on law and order". He presented the Violent Crime Control Law Enforcement Act of 1994, for example, which promised 100,000 new police officers and a huge injection of resources ($13.8 billion for law enforcement). This stance proved most successful with the American electorate.

Labour in opposition learned from the Democrats, competed with the Conservatives on law and order and came out with new, headline-catching rhetoric. The key slogan was 'tough on crime, tough on the causes of crime' (first used by Tony Blair in 1993 but imported from the US; Tonry, 2004). To a certain extent, policies and practices were copied from the US to the degree that some commentators spoke of a measure of 'convergence' on law and order. Private prisons were opened, sentences became stiffer, the prison population rose to new heights and there was an emphasis on 'disorder' and punitiveness (Tonry, 2004).

The police, who had been subjected to unrelenting pressure to improve their performance under the Conservatives, found no respite under New Labour. For 20 years, there has been a constant demand from central government for the police to work more effectively on their 'core business', defined as bringing crime down by concentrating on 'catching crooks' (Leishman et al, 1996). A barrage of directives emanated from the Home Office under Thatcher's regime, but under Blair and New Labour they also came from Downing Street and the Cabinet Office (and, indeed, from a bevy of Ministries; Neyroud, 2004). The central state was pressuring its police force into more effective action, with increasingly detailed and demanding proposals on crime control.

One of the soundbites New Labour picked up and used was 'zero tolerance'. The media were considered vitally important by Labour and the new government was highly conscious of dominating the media to get its message across. Shadow Home Secretary Jack Straw had visited New York in 1995 and had met Bratton and Maple. Tony Blair vocally supported zero tolerance shortly before taking office as Prime Minister of a new Labour government in 1997: 'Blair opts for zero tolerance' and 'Support for "zero tolerance": "Clear beggars from streets" says Blair' (Bowling, 1999, p 531).

Jones and Newburn (2004), however, question the 'convergence' idea by showing that attempts to introduce policies from the US in three areas were not especially successful. The areas were private prisons, sex offender registration and ZTP. Our concern is with the latter.

To explain its mixed reception in the UK, it is necessary to step back to the Brixton riots of 1981. Brixton was an inner-city area that was ethnically highly diverse. It became associated with aggressive street crime and in response the Metropolitan Police (the Met) introduced Operation Swamp 81, a high-visibility effort to 'swamp' the area with uniformed officers who applied strict enforcement with so-called 'stop-and-search' tactics. It was effectively a forerunner of what was later dubbed zero tolerance. This tough intervention brought the police into confrontation with predominantly black youths and serious rioting broke out on a scale rarely seen until then in the UK outside of Northern Ireland. Lord Scarman (1981) held an investigation into the disturbances and, in essence, he argued that the police should police with the consent of the public, should invest in community relations and should avoid provocative operations that carried the danger of escalation.

In a way, this was a restatement of the traditional values of the British police and the senior officers who came to the top in the post-Scarman era took his views on board. In fact, by the end of the 1980s, an elite of 'liberal-minded' chiefs had emerged at the top of the police organisation (Reiner, 1991). Senior officers were now thought to be multiskilled, geared to management tasks, multi-agency cooperation and the media, and no longer fixated solely on crime control. This perhaps helps to explain why ZTP was introduced in Britain largely as a tactical, short-term measure in contrast to the rigour of New York (Hopkins Burke, 1998).

There had been visits to New York by members of Her Majesty's Inspectorate of Constabulary and senior officers from a number of forces including the Met – Met officers were sceptical but came back 'converted' – and Bratton and Maple had both been invited to come and advise UK forces (Jones and Newburn, 2007). Indeed, when David Blunkett was Home Secretary, he paraded around with Bratton. However, when ZTP was introduced in the King's Cross area of London, for instance, it was as a short-lived clean-up in the vicinity of the three railway stations in the area to remove prostitutes, drug users, homeless and other street people. On the one hand, this was plainly allied to a major redevelopment of the area while, on the other hand, the local police along with the transport police distanced themselves from the New York model. The language was that no offence, 'however trivial', would be tolerated, but the initiative was viewed not so much as new but more as one in a series of 'logically related' operations that began in 1994 (Geleijnse, 1997, p 37). The danger with this type of tactic is that it leads only to dispersion and that any relaxation of effort results in a return of the inhabitants of such inner-city enclaves. In fact, a local council report concluded later that, despite all the efforts of a dedicated team backed with extra CCTV cameras, street crime had inexorably returned to the King's Cross area: 'Britain's most expensive and well-publicised crackdown on drug-induced crime is failing' (Goodchild, 1999, p 4). In Strathclyde, the police also engaged in a clean-up operation against street crime, especially drunkenness and late-night disorder, known as Operation Spotlight, but swiftly denied that it was ZTP when that term was applied by the media. The closest example to the American ZTP model was in Cleveland under the local commander for Hartlepool, Ray Mallon, with attempts to implement POP and a sort of Compstat (Dennis, 1997).

Mallon achieved early success with rigorous enforcement against a number of offences, especially burglary. He attracted media attention and was referred to as 'Robocop Ray' (after the part-human, part-robot law enforcer in the film Robocop). He was one of the 'few British police officers of any seniority to have embraced the idea' and his view was that zero tolerance meant 'the police would return "peace to the streets" by controlling minor situations' (Jones and Newburn, 2007, p 109). Although he claimed that his ideas on policing were formed well before the New York model emerged, and were simply sound 'back to basics' policing, he was associated with ZTP when he appeared in a television documentary with Bratton. He was subsequently discredited within his force by a disciplinary investigation against him, although he claimed his admission of guilt was merely the swiftest way of leaving the police in order to take part in mayoral elections. Some saw him as too arrogant and his policies as a way of seeking short-term success while proving eventually to be counterproductive. This echoed criticism that ZTP tips the balance in policing and control towards repression (Hopkins Burke, 1998). Indeed, a number of chief officers have expressed this opinion to me. An indicator that his electoral message struck a populist cord, enthused by 'tough on crime' rhetoric and policies, came when Mallon was elected Mayor of Huddersfield.

In summarising the British experience, Jones and Newburn (2004, pp 133-4) maintain that there is little evidence of policy transfer from America in the three areas of criminal justice they examined. With regard to ZTP, it had varying definitions in different places, met 'cultural resistance' and went 'against the dominant model of policing in the UK'. Jones and Newburn conclude that 'in practice, zero tolerance has barely been copied at all in the UK'. There were 'very clear historical and political reasons why there was in fact considerable resistance to such approaches to policing ... at the time talk of "zero tolerance" reached British shores in the mid-1990s most senior police officers were against the use of the tactics associated with such an approach'. Indeed, the Chief Constable of Thames Valley, Charles Pollard, viewed by many as a liberal and highly influential police leader, was scathing in his attack on ZTP (Pollard, 1997). American punitiveness had emerged from political and economic 'neoliberalism' married to fundamental and authoritarian conservatism; this was not always echoed enthusiastically in the more liberal European countries. Generally, in Britain, practitioners did not go in for crude 'clean-sweep' operations, but made distinctions between groups and cooperated with other agencies. In the Westminster district of London, for instance, the authorities make a distinction between the 'social care agenda' (the vulnerable and socially excluded) and the 'enforcement agenda' (aimed at aggressive begging, incivilities and public drunkenness) (Paul Rock, Personal communication). This more balanced approach also holds for Australia:

> In contrast [to the US] Australian society retains (despite growing challenges) a commitment to a broader state capacity in welfare and public health and to inclusive policies of multiculturalism and reconciliation. (Dixon, 2005, p 489)

In the UK, ZTP was adopted to a certain extent by Labour, particularly with regard to attitudes to criminals and punishment and in new legislation (Tonry, 2004), but Jones and Newburn (2004) observe that what travelled the Atlantic more successfully was the ideology, the ideas and the rhetoric behind it. ZTP, in a world of style, rebranding, spin and soundbites, had a primarily 'symbolic function'.

If ZTP did not take root in the UK, the country closest in many ways to the US, how did it fare in the progressive, 'tolerant' Netherlands? Were zero tolerance policies introduced 'tentatively and selectively' as in certain other European countries (Karstedt, 2004, p 25)?

Transfer to the Netherlands

'From the sixties until deep into the eighties an atmosphere prevailed that everything should be possible ["*alles moet kunnen*"]. In this situation there was no room for the authority of the police. It wasn't until the nineties that the public started to ask; can't there be an end to this nonsense? But after years and years of turning a blind eye ["*gedogen*"] and of letting it go, you can't just win back authority in a week…. We had let things slide, because there was no demand for authority.' (Police commissioner, cited in Boin et al, 2003, p 117)

In the period after the Second World War, the Netherlands was characterised by sober reconstruction and conventional values. Policing was traditional, reactive and bureaucratic. Then Dutch society reacted to the turbulence of the 1960s with a sudden leap to the left (Verbij, 2005). Politicians and others were often highly progressive and policies were lenient, notably on drugs and prostitution. This fostered a pattern of selective law enforcement that came to be seen as a facet of Dutch 'tolerance'. The progressivism had a strong anti-authoritarian, egalitarian and at times anarchistic thrust and this societal shift proved traumatic for the police; indeed, they were a major target for the anarchistic youth movement known as the *Provos*. The heyday of trendy liberalism that followed was conveyed by the catch phrase 'anything goes', with a sense that almost anything should be possible (*alles moet kunnen*). The widespread challenge to traditional authority also had an impact on the police and there emerged a new generation of critical young officers kicking against the old-style system.

Three such officers in particular used a fairly technical assignment from the Ministry of the Interior to write a critical report that challenged conventional policing (POS, 1977). This argued for a more internally democratic police force and for a stronger external orientation to societal change. *A Changing Police* was concerned about the legitimacy of the police in society and about raising fundamental issues on the direction to follow, taking into account the new progressive ideology. All three authors later became influential and prominent police chiefs in leading departments (in Amsterdam, Utrecht and Haarlem): the rebels became the new establishment. The report is of central significance and it represents a genuine paradigm shift.

The call for reform had come from professionals **within the system**. And it acted for many years as a *leitmotiv* for policing in the Netherlands, giving it a strong 'social' character – geared to societal change, internal democracy and the wishes of the public. The standard style of basic policing became multiskilled teams working in specific areas, known as *gebiedsgebondenpolitiezorg* or 'area-related police service'. This echoed the wishes of politicians and policy makers:

> The revisionists wanted to break down the isolation of the police – 'imprisoned' in their own view of the world, in order to win back the confidence of the public.... In all this an important role was played by the fact that this perspective reflected the preference of administrators for a local, 'friendly' and socially embedded police. (Boin et al, 2003, pp 43-4)

From that period on, there was a series of experiments and planned change in Dutch policing. These were oriented to both internal and external change: internal efforts were geared to better communication, less hierarchy, decentralisation and problem solving; external efforts were centred on improving relations with the public, adopting a service-oriented mentality and focusing on societal problems. There were a number of key players – notably the three chiefs mentioned above, their disciples and two police researchers at the Ministry of the Interior – who spread the word by publications, by teaching at the Police Academy for future officers and by implementing the new policies in several key forces. One of the influential actors in all of this spoke of an "insider movement based on personal coalitions ... and the message was spread principally through teaching".

Of interest is that much of the conceptual content for change came from the US, and to a lesser extent the UK. A great deal was based on community-oriented policing (COP) and problem-oriented policing (POP) as well as team policing. People also drew on the research experience of the Police Foundation in Washington DC. Officers and policy makers attended conferences in the United States, visiting forces and interacting with experts on police change. Some of these experts were subsequently invited to the Netherlands in the 1980s (including Sherman, Bayley, Reiss, Bittner, Manning, Van Maanen and Kelling; Punch, 1983) Reflecting on that period, those key Dutch innovators drew on American ideas and techniques, but gave them a strong Dutch flavour with a large social and democratic component.

For Dutch society was quiet unlike American society. In fact, criminal justice in the Netherlands began to be seen as an **alternative model to the US**. In his insightful analysis of Dutch penal policy and practice, Downes (1988) showed that the judicial elite had taken professional views on rehabilitation on board collectively and believed firmly in low sentencing. Few people were imprisoned compared with the US and UK and most prisons did not have punitive regimes: indeed, in the early 1970s the number of prisoners in the Netherlands was falling and this was despite rising crime.

This alternative, progressive paradigm in criminal justice – the 'least inhumane in Europe' (Bianchi, 1975, p 1) – was viewed by outsiders as a reflection of generic Dutch 'tolerance'. One of its manifestations was selective enforcement, turning a blind eye to certain offences ('*gedogen*': Brants speaks of 'regulated tolerance', 1999). This could also take the form of non-decision making, of avoiding painful choices and rationalising the postponement of problems or even indifference (Pakes, 2004). It could be said, however, that the system was in some respects enlightened, that there was a large measure of consensus and that many politicians, policy makers and criminal justice practitioners were operating along a fundamentally different paradigm to the US. At its best, it was 'outstandingly humane', according to Downes, and it did have a considerable impact on policies and practice in criminal justice and policing (SMVP, 2004b).

But there were forces gathering that challenged that paradigm. Crime began to rise sharply from the early 1970s, with a fourfold rise between 1970 and 1983. The criminal justice system came under considerable strain, with a policy document calling for 'a drastic expansion in prison capacity' (Netherlands Ministry of Justice, 1985). The Netherlands became the centre of the European drug trade, with something of a moral panic about the rise of organised crime, and there was increasing pressure from other EU members to toughen policies (especially from France and Germany on cross-border drug traffic).

Taking this into account, it is possible in retrospect to see the Dutch police in the early 1990s at a crossroads. In research conducted in 1994-95 (SMVP, 1995; Punch et al, 1998), there appeared to be institutional insecurity, and a loss of direction and motivation. Much energy had been absorbed by a major reorganisation of the police and by the 'IRT' affair, where an Inter-regional Crime Team (or 'IRT') had used dubious methods in tackling organised crime. There was an inquiry, negative publicity and shadows over the reputations of several of the police elite, including the three architects of *A Changing Police* (Boin et al, 2003). The interviews conducted with police officers in 1994-95 (Punch et al, 1998) conveyed a somewhat battered, uninspired, rudderless agency, lacking energy and direction; there was a sense almost of malaise, of impotence with a strong desire for a new direction. The old paradigm was 'bankrupt', the time was ripe for 'fundamental change', but what was missing was a collective sense of direction (Punch et al, 1998, pp 36-7).

There was, too, an increasingly sombre picture of the criminal justice system painted in the media, highlighting prison escapes, suspects released by the courts because of technical errors and large numbers of prisoners sent home because no cells were available (SMVP, 1995). There commenced a wider debate on the defects of criminal justice and of 'tolerance' in the wider society that became increasingly sharp throughout the 1990s and culminated in a political shift to the right in the early years of this century, especially with the rise of the populist politician Pim Fortuyn (Wansink, 2004). There were feelings that people who had traditionally been associated with authority had lost that authority, that '*gedogen*' had gone too far – and had been a factor in several major disasters – and that the police had become too 'soft' (Hoogenboom and Vlek, 2002).

This has fostered a 'turnaround' on crime and safety in the past decade, with a growing emphasis on 'consistent enforcement, drawing up responsibilities far more clearly and keeping a close eye on them, revitalising public standards, letting government back in the public domain' (Hoogenboom and Vlek, 2002, p 98). It is clear that there is a determination both to eliminate the laxity, nonchalance and indifference that could characterise policing and to stimulate a more assertive and effective police apparatus. Public figures now say in retrospect that 'we had gone way too far', that tolerance had reached 'absurd proportions' and had become 'a caricature of itself' and that 'we have to abandon the fervent denial of reality' (Hoogenboom and Vlek, 2002). The downside of this, according to van Swaaningen (2004, p 1), is that 'over the last decade the Netherlands has turned into a rather intolerant, xenophobic and punitive country'.

This broad move to the right in Dutch society led to something of a struggle among police officers and others to combine the new hardness with the 'traditional' values and practices in Dutch policing from the previous two decades. In 2005, the chief of the Amsterdam Police was keen to combine a disdain for American-style zero tolerance policing (ZTP) with the new-found assertiveness. Senior officers were plainly wrestling with maintaining an emphasis on tough enforcement, while remaining mindful of a broader philosophy of providing safety for the citizen that harked back to the values of *A Changing Police* in 1977. Furthermore, the leader of the Labour Party on the city council in Amsterdam was propagating zero tolerance and quoting Tony Blair on 'tough on the causes of crime' (Punch, 2006b). He seemed to be trying to espouse toughness, while retaining the image of Amsterdam as social, tolerant and cosmopolitan.

Indeed, it is not easy to find a fervent supporter of undiluted zero tolerance in the Netherlands, but one prominent proponent can be found in the Mayor of Rotterdam, Ivo Opstelten. A strong personality from the VVD Liberal Party (which is conservative rather than liberal in the British sense), his city has major urban problems related to immigration and burgeoning street crime. In words reminiscent of Bratton in New York, Opstelten stated that: "In a large city such as Rotterdam we have to win back certain areas street by street" (cited in Hoogenboom and Vlek, 2002, p 71). When I interviewed him for my project he stated that for him zero tolerance was "take on everything; an offence is an offence; and without any warning. Not as it used to be, letting things go. Essentially, it's a consistent enforcement policy" (Punch, 2006b, p 61).

Currently, almost no Dutch police officer openly espouses zero tolerance. Crime and safety have, however, become important social and political themes in the Netherlands (SMVP, 2004a). Within the past decade, there has been a major shift in thinking; the new right spokespeople want to rid society of the shortcomings they associate with tolerance ('*gedogen*': Vlek et al, 2004). The new language reflects the 'neoliberal' thrust in New Public Management (NPM). NPM proponents speak of clear agreements (in 'contracts' or 'covenants'), setting targets, improved performance, low discretion, consistent enforcement and a fundamental determination to 'solve' problems. In this new social and political climate, traditional left thinkers have moved to the middle ground, while politicians and officials from the right have adopted this firm language and employ radical methods for vigorously tackling issues. This turnaround and its new approach had been promulgated in the Netherlands within the more neutral jargon of neoliberalism and far less in a punitive and strongly ideological rhetoric than is the case in the US and UK. Inevitably, it is a shift that has influenced the thinking and conduct of police chiefs and I will now turn to look at operational implementation in two cities influenced by ZTP.

ZTP arrives

In Utrecht city centre, a large shopping mall, Upper Catherine (UC), had become frequented by 'street people'. In 1995, the district chief had just been to the US and was most enthusiastic about ZTP. The mall straddles a busy railway station and, to allow access to the station, it is open 24 hours. This enabled it to become the refuge of street people, who hung around in groups in daytime and found shelter there at night. Pressurised by complaining shopkeepers, the mayor, Ivo Opstelten, finally decided that the 'problem' of UC had to be cleared up once and for all (this was before he was appointed as Mayor of Rotterdam – mayors are not elected in the Netherlands – and he was already displaying tough language and demanding firm enforcement).

The area police chief was keen to use ZTP in some form, but he was also familiar with the 'broken windows' concept and pursued a balance between ZTP and problem solving. He encountered three main problems. First, a clean sweep of UC would only cause displacement of the problem and it was clear that none of his police colleagues wanted it pushed on to their 'patch'. Second, a special, highly motivated police squad was set up for UC but cooperation with other agencies proved problematic. Often the formal agencies promised much on paper, but were reluctant to deliver in practice. Third, and this was related to the second problem, the street people comprised the most disadvantaged group imaginable within the advanced welfare state of the Netherlands: the homeless, the mentally ill, addicts, runaway juveniles, asylum seekers evading expulsion, and some with multiple problems. In general, they were not 'criminal'. They did not fit the picture of a dangerous underclass of 'will nots' that was so pronounced in the American literature (Kelling and Coles, 1996), but the formal agencies were not to keen to have them as clients, as they were seen as unreliable recidivists and 'losers' (although churches, voluntary agencies and charities provided some primary care).

In brief, the chief was enthused by the idea of ZTP, but it became clear that a crude crackdown would not solve the 'problem'; the answer was an opportunistic combination of ZTP, COP and POP. This fitted far more into the traditional Dutch style than undiluted ZTP. The police chief spoke of zero tolerance, but it was more a trendy term used for nuanced enforcement against certain offences in specific places and as part of a temporary answer to a broader problem.

Amsterdam is a city typified by progressive policies and by a population dedicated to habitual rule breaking and displaying disdain for authority. It has also long exemplified 'regulated tolerance' (*gedoogbeleid*), with its red-light district and drug culture. The inner city – with its bars, clubs and discos – was traditionally a difficult place to police as it was an arena for many of the 'nuisance' or 'quality of life' offences that ZTP had tackled forcefully elsewhere. This was where I started fieldwork with the Amsterdam Police, in 1974 (Punch, 1979a). I observed that it was virtually a constitutional right for Amsterdammers to ride bicycles with no lights or brakes, to ignore traffic lights and to use the streets and canals as public toilets: and the long-haired police strolled around nonchalantly and did nothing about it. When I went out with the officers, they would inform me that many activities in the area were forbidden but tolerated (for example, prostitution, brothels, gambling, opium dens). One of them said resignedly, "I'm just the zoo-keeper". By the second half of the 1990s, however, it was patently clear that the Amsterdam Police had absorbed the ZTP discourse and were determined to exert stronger control in the area and more widely in the city (van Swaaningen, 2000 & 2004).

Articles about ZTP in the US and UK had begun to appear in Dutch newspapers in 1997 and on television in 1998. Amsterdam police officers, officials, politicians and the mayor had visited New York (as had officers from other forces). There was undoubtedly a major strategic shift in the force, and the style of ZTP clearly influenced a new, assertive style of policing, although, like Mallon in Hartlepool, the police chief claimed that they were already moving in that direction before the New York model became publicised and popular. This was a noticeable cultural change from the nonchalant indifference to tackling so-called 'nuisance' offences and towards reasserting police control on the streets.

The most visible symbol of this new-style consistent enforcement against relatively minor offences was the pamphlet *Streetwise* (its title was in English). This was distributed to all officers and in an easy-to-read, pocket-book format, it detailed areas for police attention, such as excessive noise, dog droppings, garbage, tramps, graffiti, unsafe bikes and urinating in public. Each entry was accompanied by a short legal statement on the offence and the fine that could be applied on the spot. For example, on dog droppings – and *hondenpoep* had assumed prodigious proportions in the inner city – there was a short definition of the relevant legal article, which stipulated a penalty fine of 75 guilders.

There is no doubt that the police were determined to use visible and assertive patrol to 'clean up the city' in a style that echoed features of ZTP in New York and elsewhere. Significantly, officers were required to write 200 tickets a year – the thrust from the top of the force on stricter enforcement was cemented with pressure to produce. In fact, one officer is alleged to have fulfilled his quota of 200 in one day! There was notably more 'blue on the streets' (*meer blauw op straat* was a popular policy catchphrase), more attention to nuisance and disorder offences and concerted efforts to tackle inner-city dilapidation with the city council and other agencies. Large number of officers would turn out to tackle a particular offence – bikes without lights, car drivers not using seat belts, the intrusion of stalls and tables by shopkeepers and bar-owners on to pavements, and so on. At traffic lights, all cyclists would be stopped and their bikes inspected – Canute-like, one might think, but by combining enforcement with prevention, everyone could choose between an immediate fine and walking home, or having their bike mended on the spot at their own expense.

It almost appears at times as if a significant element was the determination to **motivate personnel** to take their task seriously, to improve their productivity and to take back the public domain. In this light, ZTP can perhaps be viewed as an instrument that helps motivate the front-line workers while giving the senior officers the feeling that they are back in charge.

Impact

Drawing on the experiences of Utrecht and Amsterdam and elsewhere, what can be said about the impact of ZTP in the Netherlands? From the mid-1990s onwards, Dutch police officers, civic officials and criminal justice members began to visit major cities in the US and Canada, including Baltimore, Chicago, Los Angeles, San Diego and Edmonton, but especially New York. And, as we have seen above, some elements of ZTP were adopted by several forces. In general, Dutch officials from government and public agencies are avid travellers. It is not unusual for groups of 50-60 officials to attend conferences, to go on 'working visits' or to engage in 'team-building' exercises abroad. Senior police officers have usually seen policing in major cities on several continents and use English policing expressions constantly ('hot spots', 'reassurance', 'broken windows', 'restorative justice' and so on). It is debateable, however, as to what extent these insights from abroad are really implemented. Behind the cosmopolitan façade, there are hidden conventions and, as noted, a resilient parochialism. But it is the case that some officers I spoke to had been to the US, had met Giuliani and/or Bratton, had seen Compstat in action and had come back enthused, if not, as some said, 'inspired'. There was no central governmental push for this and the initiative came from individual forces, professional groups and private agencies with little or no coordination between them.

Zero tolerance policing is a diffuse concept used by different actors in different ways and I shall focus on four main elements with regard to implementation in the Netherlands: enforcement on the streets, 'broken windows', Compstat and a new assertiveness exuding the message that the police can 'make a difference'. The level of adoption in the Netherlands varied around these four central pillars.

Enforcement on the street Assertive order maintenance patrol has been widely applied in the Netherlands in a highly selective and primarily tactical fashion (as also happened in the UK). There have certainly been no unrepentant police advocates like Mallon in Britain, but there is a distinctly more visible presence of police on the streets and far more pressure to perform than previously. The government sets targets, the chiefs accept targets – in performance contracts or 'covenants' – and, in turn, employees are set quotas for production.

'Broken windows' The metaphor was linked to decay (*verloedering*) and it reinforced, and was easily incorporated into, the existing strong emphasis on an 'integrated safety policy'. This fitted neatly within the existing paradigm of a socially involved police with partnerships with other agencies that had characterised Dutch policing for some 20 years. This term had undoubted currency and was frequently cited as influential.

Compstat This model of swift analysis of information, coupled with command accountability, has been widely adopted, albeit with no uniformity. Several chiefs saw 'intelligence-led policing' as probably the most significant feature if not the essence of contemporary policing and were most impressed with Compstat. However, the feature of pressure on senior officers to perform, in a confrontational style with outsiders present, did not conform to traditional values in Dutch policing. One chief saw it in action in New York and described it as "an incredibly tough culture, hard as nails, almost disturbing, it was management by fear" but it was also "really impressive":

> 'We thought the New York model was a good concept, and especially "IDEA" for "Information, Deployment, Effective Tactics, and Assessment". It was later used in Utrecht and Rotterdam. In South-Holland-South [his own force] we also have a version of Compstat. Once a month there is a consultation meeting, from 9-11 sharp, and the district chiefs don't know whose turn it is to present. It's all about our policy priorities – what are we solving, who are we arresting, and so on? We pay special attention to repeat offenders … we target them and it's really important to be consistent in enforcement. Either I or my deputy chairs the sessions and one of the district chiefs has to stand up and tell us about his results. It's all about results. The district chief is questioned and is confronted with reports including cuttings from the newspapers. In answering, he is supported by his management team. It's played pretty hard. This is a real cultural break for the Netherlands. In Dutch police circles it puts you in a tough spot where you can fail or else show that you can think differently. In the beginning people used to ask "Why does it have to be so tough?" and "Can't you give us more time?". But by now they have learned how to cope with it.' (Punch, 2006b, p 70)

Another said disdainfully that Compstat in New York reminded him of the Nuremberg trials. He added:

> 'We went to visit a precinct and the people there were scared; their only concern was, "How can I prepare for Compstat?". There was a female captain and the walls in her office were all covered in statistics meant for Compstat; her only concern was with these figures. That's really crazy and it casts such a shadow over your work.' (Punch, 2006b, p 76)

There has been a clear change to basing policy on the swift analysis of data. There is now pressure from the top of the organisation, with far more involvement of senior officers in operational decision making, while middle-ranking officers have become used to being called to account. However, in practice, policing is still often rooted in the renowned 'four Cs' of Dutch public culture, shaped in part by coalition politics – collegiality, consensus, compromise and conflict avoidance (Boin et al, 2003, p 197). One force, for example, built a replica of Compstat including a gallery for guests following a visit to New York. In practice, however, the meetings, known as 'POWER', were infrequent, required little preparation and were seldom followed up (Peters, 2004). Although most people expressed positive benefits in the new technique, the reality echoed the predilection for 'gezelligheid' in Dutch social life – a comforting, non-confrontational 'cosiness' – and it was absorbed into the pervasive 'overlegcultuur' or consultation culture (which drives time-conscious Anglo-Saxons, in favour of decisiveness, to despair!). Generally, Dutch institutions, with decades of industrial democracy and an ethos of egalitarianism, display a necessity to discuss issues openly and to motivate partners by involvement and not by authoritarian management. Peters (2004) also argues that the style adopted in reaction to POWER aided in maintaining the conventionally high levels of autonomy and discretion enjoyed by units and districts that were potentially threatened by the top-down approach. However, a positive by-product of the Compstat clones, according to Hoogenboom, who is currently engaged in research within several forces, is that chiefs have become far more the 'boss' in their own organisation and are more in touch with primary processes, regularly spending time with operational units and even with street patrols than in earlier periods (Personal communication).

New assertiveness A noticeable change in Dutch policing, compared with the former fairly low-key if not nonchalant style, is a new assertiveness, with a much more proactive stance in the sense of 'we can make a difference'. Contemporary police leaders have a visible presence in the community and adopt positive rhetoric in the media. And what is clear is that by mobilising more personnel for operational work, by using information more intelligently, by setting priorities to focus on specific issues ('hot spots', frequent offenders, certain offences in defined areas), and by operating closely with a range of agencies to tackle problems and emphasise prevention, the police can have an impact. This is not to underestimate the size and resilience of the issues, but in specific areas and on specific issues, the police, with their partners, are indisputably able to 'make a difference'.

Conclusion

4

'Let me assure you: any relationship between my policies and what my officers do out on the streets is purely coincidental.' (Oft-quoted ironic remark by former police chief of Rotterdam, Rob Hessing)

The architecture of policing is changing, leading to fundamental alterations in the structure, culture, functioning and accountability of the police. Yet this is occurring without any debate on policies and principles. This should be a matter of grave concern.

When the first 'bobbies' walked out on to the streets of London in 1829, they conveyed a highly symbolic message. In essence, the police agency they represented was **benign and accountable**: and its unarmed officers were ordinary citizens in uniform who would police by consent, for 'the public are the police' (Critchley, 1978). Sir Robert Peel had politically shaped this 'consent paradigm' to avoid association with the despised and feared French model of spies and a military-style *gendarmerie* under direct political control. The British model became based largely on local control and constabulary independence, with the notion that the government could not give direct operational orders while every constable was an independent law enforcement officer. From the 1960s, with the Home Office as partner, this model became known as the tripartite system. There is scope for a long debate about the validity of the image this portrays, and the reality of its workings in practice, but it is not the intention to do this here. What is clear, however, is that the domain assumptions underpinning this model have been under attack for at least two decades. Unrelenting pressure from the centre has eroded the independence of the police and brought it increasingly under government control. This is happening without a discussion of the 'big picture' – the fundamental issues driving this fundamental change. In fact, sceptics say there is no big picture.

Tighter fiscal control, a battery of directives from the Home Office and structural change are irrevocably altering policing. The contours are clear: the creation of national agencies outside of the police (for example, the Serious Organised Crime Agency, SOCA); external agencies to enhance quality (the National Policing Improvement Agency and the Policing Standards Unit); closer cooperation between the police, military and security services; national specialised policing units; possible amalgamations of forces; lateral entry; and workforce modernisation. Some speak of Trojan horses, of 'agencifying' policing (personnel in SOCA are agents without automatically holding the office of constable), of surrendering to the intelligence services and the Army and of allowing the Home Office to capture policing. One commentator dubbed the Police and Justice Bill as 'the Abolishment of Parliament Bill'; the Bill would 'give Ministers unprecedented discretionary order-making powers across the entire range of policing activities' and, according to Cramphorn (2006), this represents a centralisation of power over policing 'which has never been experienced in this county since the founding of modern policing in 1829'. One interpretation is that the police service is becoming a servile agency of the state, performing to central demands – quite the opposite of Peel's intentions. Nevertheless, the planners in Whitehall would doubtless maintain that they possessed a rational blueprint with a coherent message and a long-term vision to reform policing.

This vision, however, contradicts the body of evidence from research, journalistic analyses and political memoirs that consistently reveals that policy is determined by a multitude of variables, some personality- and faction-driven, that are not always 'rational' and coherent. For instance, some have argued that policy in the UK in recent years has been driven to a certain extent by the personal rivalry between former and current Prime Ministers Tony Blair and Gordon Brown, and that the Treasury has increasingly questioned whether or not the police service is providing 'value for money' in order to outflank the Home Office. This means that the police have to be wary of where the next 'curve ball' is coming from; for example, one chief officer told me several years ago that he used to watch out for Home Office directives, but then the 'excocets' also started coming from the Cabinet Office in Downing Street. Indeed, there is a near-bewildering accountability flow chart, not unlike the map of the London Underground, with multiple lines to and from the police (Neyroud, 2004). Commenting on it, one chief officer said to me in an interview: "It's even more complicated than that"! There are an increasing number of players, a multitude of agencies and a confusing diversity of demands.

One focal, ideological driver of policy on criminal justice has undoubtedly been a populist 'law and order' agenda that has fed political debate for some two decades. If the early New Labour motto was 'tough on crime, tough on the causes of crime,' critics maintain that we hear increasingly less of the latter. We have seen above how New Labour set out to upstage the Conservatives on law and order and to dominate the headlines. New Labour was plainly obsessed with the media and especially with getting the tabloids on its side. To take one example, when a convicted rapist serving a prison sentence won a substantial prize in a lottery, the tabloids proclaimed outrage ('Sun exposes easy life of vile lottery rapist' was the headline in *The Sun*: Perrie and Coles, 2005). Almost instantly, the Home Secretary proclaimed that he was contemplating legislation to prevent this happening again. This was patently a 'knee-jerk' reaction to the media rather than a well thought-out policy response. A similar sort of response – of politicians reacting with undue haste to high-profile media scandals – has also become evident in the Netherlands. A story about the 'toe-licker of Rotterdam', for example, who would suddenly lick women's toes in public, prompted the Minister of Justice to talk of a change in the law, as toe licking was not an offence in law.

This fixation on the media in the criminal justice arena carries the danger that government, policy makers and institutions will become co-opted, if not 'captured', by crises and moral panics (Waddington, 2007). In fact representatives of the Police Federation, assessing 10 years of Tony Blair as Prime Minister in relation to policing, focus on how Blair 'came in with guns blazing … imposing targets without consultation, introducing too much legislation, trying to force amalgamations', and especially on his short-term measures and 'knee-jerk reforms' with no long-term view of change (Haynes, 2007, p 4). While one would expect a somewhat caustic reaction from the Police Federation, Reiner (2006) provides a more balanced view, arguing that crime control policy under New Labour has been a mix of 'liberal', and evidence-based, measures as well as punitively driven proposals. Tonry (2004, p 25) is more acerbic and maintains that 'many recent criminal justice developments are better understood … as exercises in symbolic politics than as outgrowths of evidence-based policy. To a certain extent, then, criminal justice policy was shaped by instant reactions to media-fostered moral panics with headline catching sound-bites'.

This was also the case with 'zero tolerance'. It was attractive because it came from the US, and New Labour had sat at the foot of the Clinton administration when in opposition. Some commentators feel that 'British social policy in general (including crime control policy) has become increasingly "Americanised" in recent years' (Jones and Newburn, 2004, p 126). As a 'dramaturgical device', it promised an uncompromising standpoint that delivered results. This appears to be how it was utilised in France: here, there was initial opposition to the American concept, but it was then adopted by Nicolas Sarkozy when he was Minister of the Interior to bolster his tough image as crime fighter. This, in turn, helped to fuel his presidential ambitions.

But what did zero tolerance actually mean? It was a vacuous 'container' concept open to diverse interpretations, including some crude, if not sinister, ones. In a world of one-liners, it was attractive as a 'no-nonsense' label for law enforcement, getting back to that good, 'old-fashioned thief taking' so beloved of *Daily Telegraph* readers and New Labour. It has entered the political lexicon and resurfaces periodically with varying constituents: feminists, for example, have demanded zero tolerance regarding sexual harassment, with strict enforcement against, and harsh penalties for, male offenders. The Conservatives, too, have adopted it when it has suited their purpose, with Michael Howard courting Ray Mallon (who had become mayor in Hartlepool as an independent) in 2004 in order to launch a fresh assault on the Labour government, which had started to show vulnerability in the area of criminal justice (Rose, 2006). The report of the Conservatives' Police Reform Taskforce *Policing for the People* (Herbert, 2007), for example, exudes the crime control paradigm from almost every page, with zero tolerance reappearing in the guise of 'robust policing of seemingly trivial crimes'.

The zero tolerance movement from America also conveyed a predilection for a top-down management style based on results at all costs. When Bratton took over the New York City Police Department, he asked for resignation letters from all his area commanders 'in case he needed them'. This is management by intimidation. At Compstat meetings, senior officers were humiliated or even sacked on the spot in front of spectators – as if in a competitive television programme with tearful public failure as a main component. At one session in New York, a visitor from the Dutch police witnessed a precinct commander wilting under the inquisitorial barrage of the chair, Chief Anenome, who finally said to his stumbling colleague, "there's the door". He dismissed him in front of a gallery of foreign guests.

This was not far from the style that some ministers and senior civil servants adopted in Britain with the police (and other public services). There was at times an open disdain for professionals: one police chief said that "Jack Straw at least treated us as grown-ups" but others were "bullies". The then Home Secretary David Blunkett's brash treatment of David Westwood (Chief Constable of Humberside) in the wake of the Soham murder case seemed designed to humiliate him in public. Blunkett's taking of Bratton to a meeting of the Association of Chief Police Officers (ACPO) was interpreted as a calculated insult and a barely veiled threat to appoint Bratton commissioner of the Metropolitan Police if other contenders did not come up to scratch (McLaughlin, 2005). Moreover, the metaphor favoured by Whitehall, in terms of its relationship with the police – 'we steer and you row' – is demeaning to professionals.

The managerial model in all this was a crude performance culture, where senior officers had to produce and hit the targets and the lower ranks were assembly-line 'grunts' who, with low discretion, had to fulfil their quotas without murmur. As Williamson puts it (2006):

> This is not a government that can afford to slacken the pace of its public sector modernisation project. The process should dispel the cosy notion that policing in England and Wales can still be represented as a tripartite arrangement between the Home Office, local Police Authorities and Chief Constables who enjoy operational independence. We should recognise that there has been a paradigm shift. Legislation has concentrated power in the Home Secretary who sets the National Policing Plan and specifies the outcomes. In this new public management paradigm Chief Constables have an executive function only, which is *to deliver against the plan*. They are expected to aspire to nothing more grandiose than to producing the prescribed outcomes. (Emphasis added)

Chief Constables are apparently expected to abide by the traditional Dutch Army expression, 'stop chatting and keep polishing'.

The key question must be whether or not this approach is appropriate to the police service. But let us first turn the spotlight around and try to enter the thinking of the policy makers. In their haste to reform public services – in this case, the police, but also other services – they might argue that, despite intensive efforts and extra funding, the agencies have not always responded positively. They might see the police chiefs as prima donnas who promise much but return to their fiefdoms only to deviate from the agreed line because of 'local circumstances' (unless they are angling for a 'gong'.) This is certainly a complaint often heard in The Hague about the Dutch police elite, travelling around the globe, then retreating to their 'empires' and pulling up the drawbridge. There is, moreover, a lot of evidence that the police organisation is adept at evading change. This is amply illustrated in America, with Walker (2005) itemising cases where police resist reform with a near reactionary, recalcitrant and resilient malice. It should perhaps be said that, even in business corporations, organisational change projects are never unproblematic, are always 'political' and often contested, are never linear, are subject to hiccups and reversal and may eventually fail (Knights and McCabe, 2003). Above all, the lesson from institutional change is that all change brings unanticipated consequences and that the greater the change the greater the unanticipated consequences are likely to be. Boin and colleagues (2003, p 144) conclude that 'one of the most important and most uniform findings of half a century of political science research is that even implementing the most simple aims always turns out differently than anticipated'. They illustrate this with a range of studies where promising and ambitious change projects, including some in criminal justice in the area of crime control, met with disappointing and meagre results.

This echoes the results of more than 30 years of police research (Bayley, 1994; Manning, 1997a; Newburn, 2003 and 2005). Despite countless reform efforts and substantial investment in the police apparatus, research findings indicate that people at the bottom of the organisation and in specialised units frequently enjoy considerable autonomy and can successfully hinder or even undermine change efforts. Wycoff's 1982 summary of the research evidence for the US, that, 'despite all the efforts of reformers over the decades, research evidence consistently demonstrated that citizen demand shaped police work, crime-related problems constitute a small proportion of that work, and police respond to that demand in highly discretionary ways' (cited in Kelling and Coles, 1996, p 87), still largely holds true. Furthermore, there is evidence that the process of reform is slow, may be limited to one particular segment, is personality-driven and has little impact on the entire organisation (Zhao, 1996). This was often the case in the US, where the already diffuse community-oriented policing (COP) label has become utterly meaningless, covering any form of innovation, and it highly debateable as to what has been achieved with some $8 billion of federal funding (Taylor et al, 1998; Zhao et al, 1999). COP and NOP (neighbourhood-oriented policing) were often applied tentatively in the US, implemented only in certain parts of the patrol organisation, and they attracted derision from other officers. In Houston, NOP was dubbed 'no one on patrol' and elsewhere community officers were derided as 'social workers' or 'empty holster guys'; one community officer lamented to Skogan (2006, p 2) that the rest of the department 'really hates us'. Skogan himself has been associated in

Chicago with one of the most serious and prolonged efforts to implement COP in the US, with much energy being spent on eliciting citizen involvement. But, following a media scare on crime, the mayor effectively abandoned a 14-year investment in COP and appointed a hard-liner from the detective department as the new chief, who then focused on 'guns, gangs and homicides'. COP 'withered', but could not be abandoned completely, so 'there it lurks, waiting to be resurrected when a crisis of legitimacy again haunts the police, and they have to rediscover community policing in order to rebuild again their credibility with the community' (Skogan, 2006, p 10). Political expediency, slavishly following the headlines, undermined in one day a major reform project built up over many years.

Admittedly, in reform projects, there is a tendency to revert to the old ways of doing things once the initial momentum is spent, the money for innovation has been used up or a new chief arrives with another set of new ideas. The police organisation has a broad mandate, a spectrum of diffuse functions and a societal environment that is continually in movement. It is patently not that easy to achieve simple and unambiguous results in such a complex institution that is not readily steered from above (Waddington, 1999). One suspects at times that, despite the computers and custody suites, not that much has changed. .

One can, then, understand why some policy makers become impatient with the police. In 2006, after almost 10 years of reforming zeal, Prime Minister Tony Blair was still discontented and felt the criminal justice system was the public service most out of touch with the concerns of the voters. In his opinion, what was needed was a 'complete change of mindset, an avowed, articulated determination to make the protection of the law-abiding public the priority' (Allen, 2006, p 50). At the same time, we should not forget that policing represents probably one of the most essential agencies of the state because it operates visibly on the streets, impinges directly on the lives of citizens, to the extent of depriving them of their liberty and even their lives through the legitimate use of violence. It raises the most acute issues of human and civil rights and of preserving guarantees about privacy and treatment under the rule of law in civic society. Yet when we examine thinking on policing, it does appear as if there are a limited number of concepts circulating and that these continually resurface as new magic words in an institutional environment with a somewhat poor institutional memory.

I have argued that the rhetoric tends to reflect two contrasting, dichotomous 'paradigms' of policing. These I have called the 'crime control' and 'consent and service' models. The zero tolerance approach clearly opted for the former, although one has to be wary of the purveyors of double-speak, who would probably claim that it is perfectly compatible with the latter. My sense is that the crime control paradigm is difficult to combine with the consent and service model and it may well be incompatible if 'in your face' policing is propagated; Dixon and Maher (2004, p 248) refer to New South Wales where in a Sydney clone of New York's Compstat, 'it was somewhat incongruous to see a deputy commissioner who had long been an advocate of community policing demanding local commanders to promote more "in your face" policing.' But it is perhaps easier for a dominant consent approach to encapsulate crime control within its style. The danger with the tough approach is that it fosters confrontation, a repressive style and the alienation and exclusion of certain groups (New York recognised this when the police later launched a charm offensive labelled 'Courtesy, Professionalism, Respect'; Hopkins Burke, 2004, p 32). And, although this approach was tried in the UK and the Netherlands and some hard-liners did inevitably emerge, it is plain that the police elites in both countries had primarily absorbed the 'consent and service' model, with the British police adopting a consultative and rights-regarding approach.

Nevertheless, the police have increasingly become global travellers and are familiar with trends abroad. As with much policy transfer, practitioners work in a pragmatic and even opportunistic manner, filching and cannibalising ideas, filtering out those innovations that can realistically be implemented, while endeavouring to fit them into existing values and practices. British and Dutch policing was changing anyway and 'zero tolerance' simply helped to set a new tone and direction in that process. It may, then, have stimulated attention for specific processes and particular techniques that were already under way – as with intelligence-led policing (with the Kent Police as front-runners). Rather than leading to the Americanisation, or 'McDonalisation', of policing, however, zero tolerance policing was more of a passing fad in Britain with a marginal impact on an indelibly 'British' style.

For the Netherlands it is clear that a complex series of interlocking developments, domestic and international, have left their mark on Dutch policing. The pervasive community approach had become the new orthodoxy, with some new chiefs challenging it by saying it had become an end in itself; that detective work and forensics had been seriously neglected requiring that the balance be restored; and that police officers had to become figures of authority again. But compared with the uncertainty, and even tiredness, of a decade ago, there is now a new élan, more energy and self-confidence, and even pride. Following their interviews with almost all of the country's police leaders Boin and colleagues (2003, p 238) commented:

> We spoke to motivated, often still fairly ambitious and, without exception, proud people. The commitment to the organisation is high. We were told time and again that being a police chief is the best profession around.

And despite much travelling and toying with concepts from abroad, there is still a recognisable 'Dutch' policing style. It is noticeable, for instance, that the 'broken windows' concept was enthusiastically embraced because it reinforced what people had already been doing for many years. There is a degree of grappling with the 'hard cop–soft cop' dichotomy (Hopkins Burke, 2004), and, in a recent 'vision document' by police chiefs, there is an effort to marry the new assertiveness with the tradition of *A Changing Police* (Council of Commissioners, 2006). One chief that I interviewed had not come up through the traditional, predominantly male, and fairly incestuous route of the Dutch Police Academy for senior officers. To certain extent, she and others like her are bringing a broader perspective to issues:

'A young generation of chiefs has come up and as a consequence there is quite a change in composition of the Council [of Commissioners]. People are looking for a new philosophy as a replacement for "A Changing Police". Perhaps some people have gone to one extreme and they start to use a particular language, like speaking of "catching crooks" and of being "results-oriented". Certain ministers have also spoken in a rather denigrating way about the police and about the need for more "steering" of the police. But in our discussions in the Council we have to avoid arriving at either-or situations. That means not thinking one-dimensionally but trying to tackle the problem in a smart but also a business like way. The constant question has to be "how do we steer the system along the main line?" and then take strategic choices accordingly ... I'm strongly convinced that you have to seek legitimacy through the relationship you have with the public and though winning their trust. I believe we should simply focus on our core tasks – enforcement, investigation and helping those in need – in the knowledge that we just can't do everything. Of great importance is the relationship with your environment and also cooperation with others in the [criminal justice] chain, with other social services and other support agencies and with the local authorities.... The key to all this is an integrated safety policy and I believe in this most firmly. We have to draw the public towards us; they have to become our eyes and ears – and we also have to be prepared to make demands on them. Our policy and enforcement has to have an impact on norms and values. People should be made aware about which rules are being applied. We have to stand squarely behind our views and stick firmly to a clear position. We should not chase after the flavour of the month, from politicians who chase after every little incident, and we should stand up much more firmly for our views.' (Punch, 2006b, p 102)

This nuanced view contrasts with the US, where, as Dixon observes (2005, p 489) zero tolerance contained a particular vision of social order and was a policy 'designed for a society which regards criminal justice and punitiveness as its primary tools of social policy'. That is simply not the case in the Netherlands. A senior Dutch police officer is focused primarily on policing in Dutch society within an existing and long-standing Dutch policing and criminal justice paradigm. He, or she, may adopt concepts and practices from abroad, but will almost certainly see these as strengthening existing policies. There has been 'transfer' for some 30 years, but it has been a highly selective process with constant adaptation to domestic circumstances. The Commissioner of Amsterdam, for example, who was seen as a respected reflective practitioner trying to match the legacy of *A Changing Police* to the new realities, said:

'I had to laugh a bit about zero tolerance; it was very much in the spirit of the times. You get such an overemphasis on figures with Compstat and, if you only pay attention to production and results, then it will be at the expense of your professionalism. We did take over a part of zero tolerance but we have also taught ourselves to be much more selective; we don't just go along with fashions.' (Punch, 2006b, p 78)

This can perhaps lead to rationalising the non-adoption of an innovation by arguing for the specificity of the local situation and the non-applicability of the site visited. New York, for instance, may be seen as a fascinating, innovative and stimulating place to visit but, by being so radically different to any Dutch city, it is effectively on another planet. It is perhaps sociologically naïve to think that it might be otherwise.

Finally, zero tolerance was more of a rhetorical device than a major policy shift in both countries, although it has acted as a catalyst for a more assertive style of policing geared to the swift use of intelligence and a more visible police presence on the streets. Indeed, zero tolerance can be viewed less as a coherent policy and more as a 'rhetorical device' used by different parties for different ends (Jones and Newburn, 2004), while Dixon (2005, p 497) sees it as carrying 'a conservative lament about social decline'. It could even be described as a '**policy myth**'. As recently as May 2007, I was told at a meeting at the Police Federation (of England and Wales) that government officials were still pushing the New York experience as the model for successfully combating crime, as if this has been unequivocally established. This is despite the fact that Karmen (2001) demolished this claim some years back. This is related to the increasing tendency of politicians, the media and practitioners to pick up concepts and to use them rather uncritically, without any scrutiny of the evidence. According to Bowling (1999, p 548), 'we still do not know which policing strategies are most effective or why.... Part of the reason for this uncertainty is that too few policing strategies are evaluated, fewer still are evaluated properly so that others can see what works, for whom, and why'. The concepts act as taken-for-granted code words, conveying novelty or robustness and claiming a new, 'successful' approach to issues. It helps if these unexamined 'best practices' come from another country, allowing for 'policy tourism' (preferably of the transcontinental kind; Dixon and Maher, 2004, p 259). To a certain extent, then, policy has become driven by personalities, incidents, media headlines, short-term results, imported one-liners and, in criminal justice in particular, by moral panics and populism.

All this avoids concentrating on the 'big picture'. What is policing for, how does it function in a democracy and to whom are the police accountable? And, crucially, on what paradigm or philosophy is it based? That decision should illuminate the issues of control, of economies of scale, of the balance between macro agencies and local delivery, of the use of deadly force, of the relationship between the police and the military and security agencies and, vitally, of accountability at all levels (Punch and Markham, 2007). Running through that discourse should be pivotal issues related to trust, credibility, legitimacy and integrity. Can the state be trusted to protect citizens from the arbitrary use of authority (Gilmour, 2006)? Behind this is the contest over who has the power to define policing and, in that definition, what the nature of the 'contract' with the public is. It is noticeable, for instance, that there has not been a Royal Commission in the UK for some 40 years. The Police Federation has been calling for one for some years, and in June 2007 ACPO added its voice to a demand for a public debate on policing. Interestingly, Britain's leading police officer, Sir Ian Blair, made a plea in his BBC Dimbleby Lecture (2005) for a debate to ascertain 'what sort of police does the public want?'

But who is to conduct that debate, and when? In response to such a debate, the police would have to clarify its philosophy and display professionalism and unity of position (including with other stakeholders such as the police authorities and the Police Federation). This implies more sophistication in strategy formulation, scenario planning, environmental scanning (pooling knowledge on visits abroad and evaluating trends), lobbying, critical self-scrutiny, and, above all, investment in the primary processes. This is because policing is a 24-hour emergency service, driven by calls from the public and by emergency situations (disasters, civil emergencies, large-scale investigations). It relies primarily on the professional and craft skills of front-line personnel in direct interaction with the public. That interaction requires judgement, discretion, competence and respect for the citizen. ZTP and New Public Management, in contrast, try to turn front-line workers into assembly-line operatives, who are evaluated on how productive they are and not on the quality of their interaction with citizens or their problem-solving skills. As such, these managerial movements distort policing and, at worst, undermine it by destroying competences and motivation. Some senior officers share these views, and argue for an emphasis on 'public value,' but it may be too late to stem the tide.

The problem is that the landscape of policing is altering dramatically and rapidly. Will the new structure be benign, accountable and service-oriented and will it protect citizens from arbitrary authority? It is proving difficult to trace the architect of this new structure, and to uncover the blueprint, and the public is simply not being consulted. This essential agency is being reformed with indecent haste and effectively with a reversal to a 'crime control' paradigm without any fundamental public discussion, against prevailing police values and with no formally articulated, long-term vision on policing. In this light, the zero tolerance hype reveals the poverty of thinking on policy for policing: it simply means reverting to a non-reflective, ostensibly common-sense, 'business as usual', back to 'real policing' agenda, with that meaningless mantra of 'old-fashioned thief taking'. Except now the government has become the thief: and it has stolen the police from us.

References

Alderson, J. (1979) *Policing Freedom*, Plymouth: Macdonald and Evans.

Allen, R. (2006) 'Editorial: community engagement', *Criminal Justice Matters*, No 64 Summer, p 3.

Andrews, W. (1997) 'The new NYPD', htpp://onpatrol.com

Audit Commission (1993) *Helping with Enquiries: Tackling Crime Effectively*, London: HMSO.

Bayley, D.H. (1994) *Police for the Future*, New York/Oxford: Oxford University Press.

Bayley, D.H. (2006) 'Police reform: who done it?', Paper presented at Police Reform from the Bottom-Up Conference, University of California, Berkeley: CA, 12-13 October.

Bayley, D.H. and Shearing, C. (2001) *The New Structure of Policing*, Washington, DC: National Institute of Justice.

Beusekamp, W. (2004) 'Een sociaal New York, dat moet Amsterdam worden / A sociable New York, that's what Amsterdam should be', *de Volkskrant*, 23 September, p 3.

Bianchi, H. (1975) 'Social control and deviance in the Netherlands', in H. Bianchi et al (eds) *Deviance and Control in the Netherlands*, London: Wiley.

Blair, I. (2003) 'Leading towards the future', Speech at Future of Policing Conference, London School of Economics, London, 10th October.

Blair, I. (2005) Richard Dimbleby Lecture, BBC, London, 16th November.

Boin, R.A., van de Torre, E.J. and Hart, P. (2003) *Blauwe Bazen: Het Leiderschap van Korpschefs / Blue Bosses: The Leadership of Police Chiefs*, Zeist: Kerkebosch.

Bowling, B. (1996) 'Broken windows theory', Presentation for Home Office, London, November 28th.

Bowling, B. (1999) 'The rise and fall of New York murder', *British Journal of Criminology*, vol 39, no 4, pp 531-54.

Bowling, B. and Ross, J. (2006) 'SOCA: the Serious Organised Crime Agency', *Criminal Justice Matters*, No. 63, Spring, pp 8-9, 36.

Brants, C. (1999) 'The fine art of regulated tolerance: prostitution in Amsterdam', *Journal of Law and Society*, vol 25, no 4, pp 621-53.

Bratton, W. (1997) 'Crime is down in New York: blame the police', in N. Dennis (ed) *Zero Tolerance: Policing a Free Society*, London: Institute for Economic Affairs.

Bratton, W. with Knobler, P. (1998) *Turnaround: How America's Top Cop Reversed the Crime Epidemic*, New York, NY: Random House.

Brogden, M. (2005) '"Horses for courses" and "thin blue lines": community policing in transitional society', *Police Quarterly*, vol 8, no 1, pp 64-98.

Business Week (1993) 'The economics of crime', 13 December, pp 42-8.

Chan, J. (1997) *Changing Police Culture: Policing in a Multicultural Society*, Melbourne: Cambridge University Press.

Christie, N. (2000) *Crime Control as Industry* (3rd edn), London: Routledge.

Clare, P. (1998) 'Managing change', *Criminal Justice Matters*, No. 32 Summer, pp 9-11.

Council of Commissioners (2006) *The Police in Evolution: Vision on Policing* (2006), The Hague: Dutch Police Institute.

Cramphorn, C. (2006) 'Whitehall set for an unfair cop,' *Yorkshire Post*, 24 March, p 5.

Critchley, T.A. (1978) *A History of Police in England and Wales*, London: Constable.

Dennis, N. (ed) (1997) *Zero Tolerance: Policing a Free Society*, London: Institute for Economic Affairs.

Dixon, D. (2005) Beyond zero tolerance', in T. Newburn (ed) *Policing: Key Readings*, Cullompton: Willan.

Dixon, D. and Maher, L. (2004) 'Containment, quality of life and crime reduction: policy transfers in the policing of a heroin market', in T. Newburn and R. Sparks (eds) *Criminal Justice and Political Cultures*, Cullompton: Willan, pp 234-66.

Downes, D. (1988) *Contrasts in Tolerance*, Oxford: Clarendon Press.

Downes, D. and Morgan, R. (1997) 'Dumping the "hostages to fortune"? The politics of law and order in post-war Britain', in M. Maguire, R. Morgan and R. Reiner (eds) *The Oxford Handbook of Criminology*, Oxford: Clarendon Press, pp 87-134.

Ericson, R.V. and Haggerty, K.D. (1997) *Policing the Risk Society*, Oxford: Oxford University Press.

Fitzgerald, M., Hough, M., Joseph, I. and Qureshi, T. (2002) *Policing for London*, Cullompton: Willan.

Geleijnse, H. (1997) 'Nee tegen anti-sociaal gedrag' / 'No to anti-social behaviour', *de Volkskrant*, 11 January, p 37.

Gilmour, S. (2006) 'Why we trussed the police', Unpublished Masters thesis, Centre of Criminology, University of Oxford.

Goldstein, H. (1979) 'Improving policing: a problem oriented approach', *Crime and Delinquency*, 25, April pp 236-158.

Goodchild, S. (1999) 'King's Cross vice defies the cameras', *The Independent on Sunday*, 22 August, p 4.

Greene, J.A. (1999) 'Zero tolerance: a case study of police policies and practices in New York', *Crime and Delinquency*, vol 45, no 2, pp 171-87.

Haynes, C. (2007) 'Ten years of Tony', *Police Review*, vol 115, 22 June, pp 4, 8-21.

Herbert, C. (2007) *Policing for the People: Interim Report of the Police Reform Taskforce*, London: Conservative Party.

Hinton, M.S. (2006) *The State on the Streets*, Boulder, CO/London: Lynne Reiner Publishers Inc.

Hoogenboom, B. and Vlek, F. (eds) (2002) *Gedoogbeleid: tolerantie en poldermodel: tellen (we) onze zegingen Nog?/ Blind-eye policy: tolerance and the polder model: can we still count our blessings?*,, Zeist: Kerkebosch/Apeldoorn: Politie en Wetenschap.

Hopkins Burke, R. (1998) *Zero Tolerance Policing*, Leicester: Perpetuity Press.

Hopkins Burke, R. (2004) *Hard Cop, Soft Cop: Dilemmas and Debates in Contemporary Policing*, Cullompton: Willan.

Hornberger, J. (2007) "'Don't push this constitution down my throat": human rights in everyday practice'. An ethnography of police transformation in Johannesburg, South Africa', Draft PhD thesis, University of Utrecht.

Johnson, S. (1998) *Who Moved My Cheese?*, New York: Putnam Adult.

Johnston, P. and Steele, J. (2000) 'Chasing criminals? That's not their job',*The Daily Telegraph*, 17 May, p 4.

Jones, T. and Newburn, T. (1998) *Private Security and Public Policing*, Oxford: Oxford University Press.

Jones, T. and Newburn, T. (2004) 'The convergence of US and UK crime policy: exploring substance and process'', in T. Newburn and R. Sparks (eds) *Criminal Justice and Political Cultures*, Cullompton: Willan.

Jones, T. and Newburn, T. (2007) *Policy Transfer and Criminal Justice*, Maidenhead: Open University Press.

Karmen, A. (2001) *New York Murder Mystery: The True Story Behind the Crime Crash of the 1990s*, New York, NY: New York University Press.

Karmen, A. (2004) 'Zero tolerance in New York city', in R. Hopkins Burke (ed) *Hard Cop, Soft Cop: Dilemmas and Debates in Contemporary Policing*, Cullompton: Willan.

Karstedt, S. (2004) 'Durkheim, Tarde and beyond: the global travel of crime policies', in T. Newburn, T. and R. Sparks (eds) *Criminal Justice and Political Cultures*, Cullompton: Willan.

Kelling, G.L. and Coles, C.M. (1996) *Fixing Broken Windows*, New York, NY: Free Press.

Knights, D. and McCabe, D. (2003) *Guru Schemes and American Dreams*, Maidenhead: Open University Press.

Kraska, P. (ed) (2001) *Militarising the American Criminal Justice System*, New York, NY: New York University Press.

Lardner, J. (1997) 'Can you believe the New York miracle?', *New York Review of Books*, 14 August, pp 54-8.

Leigh, A., Read, T. and Tilley, N. (1996) *Problem-oriented Policing: Brit Pop*, London: Home Office.

Leishman, F., Savage, S. and Loveday, B. (1996) (eds) *Core Issues in Policing*, London: Longman.

Loader, I. (2004) 'Policing, securitisation and democratisaton in Europe', in T. Newburn and R. Sparks (eds) *Criminal Justice and Political Cultures*, Cullompton: Willan.

Loveday, B. (1996) 'Crime at the core?', in F. Leishman, B. Loveday and S. Savage (eds) *Core Issues in Policing*, London: Longman.

Loveday, B. and Reid, A. (2003) *Going Local*, London: Policy Exchange.

Macpherson, Sir W. of Cluny (1999) *The Stephen Lawrence Inquiry*, London: HMSO.

Manning, P.K. (1977) *Police Work*, Cambridge, MA: MIT Press.

Manning, P.K. (1997a) *Police Work* (2nd edn), Prospect Heights, IL: Waveland Press.

Manning, P.K. (1997b) 'Community Policing, Broken Windows and Zero Tolerance Policing,' Paper presented at conference on Zero Tolerance, Henry Fielding Centre, Manchester University, 25 March.

Marks, M. (2005) *Transforming the Robocops*, Scottsville, South Africa: University of KwaZulu-Natal Press.

McLaughlin, E. (2005) 'Forcing the Issue: New Labour, New Localism and the Democratic Renewal of Police Accountability', *The Howard Journal*, 44, 5, pp 473-489.

Mollen Commission (1994) *Report of the Commission to Investigate Allegations of Police Corruption and the Anti-corruption Procedures of the Police Department*, New York, NY: City of New York

Montgomery, L. (1997) 'Broken windows: how a theory shook the foundations of law enforcement and helped heal a city', http://onpatrol.com

Moore, M.H. (2005) 'Sizing up Compstat: an important administrative innovation in policing', in T. Newburn (2005) (ed) *Policing: Key Readings*, Cullompton: Willan.

Morgan, R. and Newburn, T. (1997) *The Future of Policing*, Oxford: Oxford University Press.

Nadelman, E. (1993) *Cops Across Borders*, University Park, PA: Pennsylvania State University Press.

Netherlands Ministry of Justice (1985) *Society and Crime: A Policy Plan for the Netherlands*, The Hague: Netherlands Ministry of Justice.

Newburn, T. (ed) (2003) *Handbook of Policing*, Cullompton: Willan.

Newburn, T. (ed) (2005) *Policing: Key Readings*, Cullompton: Willan.

Newburn, T. and Sparks, R. (eds) (2004) *Criminal Justice and Political Cultures*, Cullompton: Willan.

Neyroud, P. (2004) 'Closer to the citizen? Developing accountability and governance in policing', Paper presented at the British Society of Criminology Conference, Birmingham, September.

Pakes, F. (2004) 'The politics of discontent: the emergence of a new criminal justice discourse', *The Howard Journal*, vol 43, no 3, pp 284-98.

Patten Report (1999) *A New Beginning: Policing in Northern Ireland. Report of the Independent Commission on Policing for Northern Ireland*, London: Home Office.

Perrie, R. and Coles, J. (2005) 'Lotto rapist found', *The Sun*, 30 September, pp 4-7.

Peters, A. (2004) 'POWER in Brabant-Noord', Unpublished Masters thesis, University of Twente.

Peters, T.J. and Waterman, R.H. (1982) *In Search of Excellence: Lessons from America's Best-Run Companies*', New York, NY: Harper and Row.

Policing in the Netherlands (2004) report available from the Police Department of the Ministry of the Interior in The Hague.

Pollard, C. (1997) 'Zero tolerance: short-term fix, long-term liability?', in N. Dennis (ed) *Zero Tolerance: Policing a Free Society*, London: Institute for Economic Affairs.

POS (Projectgroep Organisatie Structuren) (1977) *Politie in Verandering / A Changing Police*, The Hague: Staatsuitgeverij.

Punch, M. (1979a) *Policing the Inner City*, London: Macmillan.

Punch, M. (1979b) 'The secret social service', in S. Holdaway (ed) *The British Police*, London: Edward Arnold.

Punch, M. (ed) (1983) *Control in the Police Organization,* Cambridge, MA: MIT Press.

Punch, M. (1985) *Conduct Unbecoming: The Social Construction of Police Deviance and Control*, London: Tavistock

Punch, M. (2006a) *Van 'Alles Mag' Naar 'Zero Tolerance': Policy Transfer en de Nederlandse Politie / From 'Anything Goes' to 'Zero Tolerance': Policy Transfer and the Dutch Police,* Apeldoorn: Programma Politie en Wetenschap / Police Research Programme.

Punch, M. (2006b) 'From "anything goes" to "zero tolerance": policy transfer and the Dutch police', Unpublished translation of Punch (2006a).

Punch, M. and Markham, G. (2007) 'Embracing accountability', forthcoming in *Policing: A Journal of Policy and Practice.*

Punch, M., van der Vijver, K. and van Dijk, N. (1998) *Searching for a Future,* Dordrecht: SMVP. (translation of SMVP (1995) *Toekomst Gezocht:* Dordrecht: SMVP).

Reiner, R. (1991) *Chief Constables: Bobbies, Bosses or Bureaucrats?,* Oxford: Oxford Oxford University Press.

Reiner, R. (1997) 'Policing and the police', in M. Maguire, R. Morgan and R. Reiner (eds) *The Oxford Handbook of Criminology,* Oxford: Clarendon Press.

Reiner, R. (2000) *The Politics of the Police* (3rd edn), Oxford: Oxford University Press.

Reiner, R. (2006) 'Law and order – a 20:20 vision', in J. Holder and C. O'Cinneide (eds) *Current Legal Problems,* Oxford: Oxford University Press, pp 129-60.

Remnick, D. (1997) 'The crime buster', *The New Yorker,* 24 February, pp 94-102.

Ritzer, G. (1997) *The McDonaldization of Society,* Thousand Oaks, CA: Pine Forge Press.

Rock, P. (1978) *The Making of Symbolic Interactionism,* London: Macmillan.

Rose, D. (2006) 'Crime rate soars as criminals walk free', *The Observer on Sunday,* 28 May, p 3.

Scarman, Lord (1981) *The Scarman Report,* Harmondsworth: Penguin.

Silverman, E. (1999) *NYPD Battles Crime: Innovative Strategies in Policing,* Boston, MA: Northeastern University Press.

Skogan, W. (2006) 'Why reforms fail,' Paper presented at the Police Reform from the Bottom-Up Conference, University of California, Berkeley, CA, 12-13 October.

Smith, G. (2004) 'What's law got to do with it? Some reflections on the police in the light of developments in New York City', in R. Hopkins Burke (ed) *Hard Cop, Soft Cop: Dilemmas and Debates in Contemporary Policing,* Cullompton: Willan.

Smolowe, J. (1993) 'America the violent', *Time International* 23 August, pp 15-21.

SMVP/Stichting Maatschappij Veiligheid en Politie (1995) *Toekomst Gezocht/ Searching for a Future* Dordrecht: SMVP / Dutch Police Foundation for Society and Safety.

SMVP/Stichting Maatschappij Veiligheid en Politie (2004a) *Klem van Gedogen/ Trapped in Tolerance,* Dordrecht: SMVP. Dutch Police Foundation for Society and Safety.

SMVP Stichting Maatschappij Veiligheid en Politie (2004b) *Stichting Maatschappij, Veiligheid en Politie 18 Jaar (1986-2004) / The Dutch Police Foundation for Society and Safety 18 years (1986-2004),* Dordrecht: SMVP. Dutch Police Foundation for Society and Safety.

Stenning, P. (2000) 'Power and accountability in private policing', *European Journal of Criminal Policy and Research*, vol 8, no 3), pp 325-52.

Swaaningen, R., van (2000) 'Tolerance or zero tolerance: is that the question?' Paper presented to the American Society of Criminology Conference, Washington, DC, November.

Swaaningen, R., van (2004) 'Public safety and management of fear,' Paper presented to the European Society of Criminology Conference, Amsterdam, September.

Taylor, R. W., Fritsch, E. J. and Caeti, T. J. (1998), 'Core challenges facing community policing: The emperor *still* has no clothes', *ACJS Today*, vol XVII, issue I, May / June, pp 1-5.

The Economist (1993) 'Hell is an American city', 6 November, pp 11-12.

Tilley, N. (2003) 'Community policing, problem-oriented policing and intelligence-led policing' in T. Newburn, T. (ed) *Handbook of Policing*, Cullompton: Willan, pp 311-99.

Tonry, M. (2004) *Punishment and Politics*, Cullompton: Willan.

Tyler, T. R. and Huo, Y. J. (2002) *Trust in the Law*, New York: Russell Sage Foundation.

Verbij, A. (2005) *Tien Rode Jaren / Ten Red Years* , Amsterdam: Ambo.

Vijver, van der, K. (2004) 'De functie en gezag van de politie' / 'The function and authority of the police', in J. Kuiper et al (eds) *Rust'loos Wakend / Uneasy Guardianship,* Amsterdam: Regiopolitie Amsterdam-Amstelland.

Vlek, F., Bangma, K., Loef, K. and Muller, E. (eds) (2004) *Uit Balans: Politie en Bestel in de Knel / Out of Balance: Police and System in a Tight Spot*, Zeist: Kerkebosch.

Waddington, P.A.J. (1999) *Policing Citizens*, London: UCL Press.

Waddington, P.A.J. (2007) 'Police service must play it by ear', *Police Review*, vol.115, 22 June, pp 14-15.

Walker, S. (2005) *The New World of Police Accountability*, Thousand Oaks, CA: Sage Publications.

Wansink, H. (2004) *De Erfenis van Fortuyn / The Heritage of Fortuyn*, Amsterdam: Meulenhoff.

Weisbrud, D., Mastrofski, S.D., McNally, A M., Greenspan, R. and Willis, J. (2005) 'Reforming to preserve: Compstat and strategic problem solving in American policing', in T. Newburn (ed) *Policing: Key Readings*, Cullompton: Willan.

Williamson, T. (2006) 'Who needs police authorities?', *Police Review*, vol 114, 20 January, p 15.

Wilson, J.Q. and Kelling, G. (1982) 'Broken windows: the police and neighbourhood safety', *The Atlantic Monthly*, vol 249, no 3, pp 29-38.

Zhao, J. (1996) *Why Police Organizations Change*, Washington, DC: Police Executive Research Forum.

Zhao, J., Lovrich, N.P. and Thuman, Q. (1999) 'The status of community policing in American cities', *Policing: International Journal of Police Science & Management*, vol 22, no 1, pp 74-91.

Appendix: The Dutch police*

The Dutch police is organised into 25 regional forces and one national police agency (KLPD). The forces range from the largest (Amsterdam-Amstelland, with roughly 6,000 personnel), to the smallest, with under 600 officers. There are approximately 37,000 officers in the 26 forces, with about 15,000 other employees. The Ministry of the Interior is primarily responsible for the police, but the Ministry of Justice retains responsibility for the investigation and prosecution of crimes. In the regions, the commissioner (*hoofdcommissaris*) defers to the force manager (*korpsbeheerder*), who is the mayor of the largest city and primarily in charge of the police, and to the Chief Public Prosecutor on criminal investigations. The regional chief meets regularly with his or her two 'bosses' in the 'triangular' consultations on policy and enforcement and both can take decisions effecting operational issues. The 26 chiefs meet monthly in the Council for Chief Commissioners (*Raad van Hoodfcommissaren*), which does not take binding decisions. Unlike the Association of Chief Police Officers in the UK, only the 26 chiefs take part and no other high-ranking officers (the 'chief officers' in the UK).

* For more details, see *Policing in the Netherlands* (2004), available from the Police Department of the Ministry of the Interior in The Hague.